EVALUATING FOR EXCELLENCE

Teresa M. Moon

BEAUTIFUL FEET BOOKS
Sandwich, Massachusetts

ISBN 1-893103-04-8

Formerly published as
How Do You Know They Know What They Know?
Grove Publishing
1997

Published by Beautiful Feet Books
139 Main Street
Sandwich, MA 02563

www.bfbooks.com
508-833-8626

Acknowledgments

Is it really possible to thank everyone who contributed to an idea-sharing tool such as this? I am certain it is not, but I wish to do the best job I can of recognizing at least a few of the individuals who generously gave of their time and talents.

First, I must give all honor and thanks to my Lord and Savior who has taught me much about what is of *value* and of *worth* and what will stand the true test of time and of fire.

Next, I wish to thank my husband, David, whose idea it was that I compile these pages and with whose encouragement and support I have finally completed this project. I must also thank my children, Wendell and Devin, for providing much of the material for the content as well as giving me a reason to consider what is of value. I thank them all for their patience with me during this adventure!

Thanks also to Debe Haller and Mary Harrington for their many suggestions to help make this tool more user friendly for you. I cannot thank Michael Allen enough for the many silly computer questions he has answered and for his tremendous problem-solving abilities.

Many thanks, as well, to the families of Harvest Christian Academy and to parents who have attended my workshops and for voicing their questions and concerns about evaluating the education of their children. Many of them have prompted the forms you find in these pages.

Table of Contents

Introduction	1
Model for Teaching and Evaluating	5
DIAGNOSE	9
Prepare to Diagnose/Using Diagnostic Tools	11
Educator's Objectives	14
Educator's Diagnostic Survey	15
Suggested Scope and Sequence	16
Diagnostic Reading Checklist	21
Student Reading Inventory	23
Diagnostic Writing Checklist	24
Student Writing Inventory	26
Diagnosing Writing Skills	27
Writing Prompts	28
Student Writing Sample	30
Observation Notes	31
Informal Handwriting Assessment	35
Character Qualities Review	36
Student Inventory	37
PLAN	39
Props for Projecting/Using Projecting Tools	41
Individualized Education Program (IEP)	42
IEP General Information Form	45
IEP Student Success Study Team	46
IEP Annual Goals and Methods	47
IEP Special Education	49
Educator's Objectives Sample	50
Objectives and Evaluation Form	51
Junior and Senior High Level Writing Assignments	53
Physical Education Record	54
GUIDE	55
Guidelines That Gauge/Using Guiding Tools	57
Oral Presentation Student Guidelines	59
Format for One-Page Essay	60
Writing Guidelines	62
Guidelines to Critique Writing	63
Sample Writing Assignment	64

Table of Contents

Science Project Student Timeline	65
Student Project Timeline	66
Public Speaking Course Outline	67
Course Outline: Music	68
Reading Comprehension	69
Book Project Ideas	71
Approved Book List	75
Reading Genres	76
Independent Reading Contract	78
Book Projects	79
Literature Project	80
Math Skills Checklist	81
EVALUATE	83
Tools to Evaluate	85
Portfolio Assessment	86
Creating a Portfolio	87
Portfolio Samples	90
Handwriting Critique	95
Writing Mechanics and Punctuation	96
Writng Critique	99
Public Speaking Evaluation for Individual Presentations	100
Public Speaking Course Evaluation	101
Research Project Evaluation	102
Geography Unit Study	103
Map Guidelines	104
Poetry Reading/Recitation Evaluation	105
Science Project Evaluation	106
Math Records	107
Reference Materials	110
PULLING IT ALL TOGETHER	111
Getting the Most out of this Book	113
A Place to Begin	115
Oral Presentation Critique	118
Sample Forms Use Guide	119
Critical Thinking	121
GLOSSARY	127
APPENDIX - See Forms Index beginning on p. 197	131

 # Introduction

I would like to introduce myself to you and also explain the purpose for this book by sharing with you the following true story. I believe it will help you get to know me a little bit, and more importantly, see why I am convinced the information and tools shared in these pages are so necessary for our consideration as parents.

Come with me to a day that my family nostalgically refers to as "Devin's Day." It had been "one of those weeks." Home schooling magazines, newsletters, and other correspondence had piled up on the coffee table, never having been opened. I was looking forward to this moment when I would have some time to sit on the couch and leaf through the pile, hoping for some encouragement. I don't remember actually reading anything, but I do remember waking up to a scream.

"Devin's hurt!" yelled my older son, Wendell, running through the patio door. Well, Devin's always hurt. I didn't even get up. I calmly remained in my reclined position. "Devin's bleeding!" came the frantic reply. Devin is always bleeding. It is still no cause for alarm. I didn't budge.

Next Devin came through the door . . . bleeding! Have you ever experienced that moment of panic when your mind races between "This is an emergency" and "Don't get blood on my sofa?" This *was* an emergency. Now I jumped.

Fortunately, I had the presence of mind to grab clean towels. He was losing a lot of blood. I told Wendell to grab my keys. I looked out the kitchen window while applying pressure to the wound and realized we weren't going anywhere. We live on a very busy street between two high schools, one public, one private. The evening before there had been a football game, and someone had thrown a rock through the rear window of our van. The interior of the van was covered with shattered glass.

I called a friend who was in the middle of a bridal shower. She sent her husband to chauffeur us to the hospital. He asked if I shouldn't leave a note for my husband. I responded that when he got home and saw all this blood, my husband would have to know where we were. On the way to the hospital, we passed my husband. We honked and waved. He honked and waved and drove on home. When he walked in the house, he went straight to the TV and turned on the football game, not noticing anything out of place.

We called from the hospital to invite him to join in the fun. As soon as he hung up the phone, he heard a screeching sound from the boys' room. When he entered, the boys' hamster was sprawled, trembling, in the middle of the floor. He soon realized the kitten had gotten his head stuck in the tunnel of the hamster's habit trail and was flailing about making horrible noises in an attempt to free himself. He later told me that seeing the cat with eyes bugging out and ears plastered back, it had occurred to him that a video of this scene could prove quite profitable. Surely, *Funniest Home Videos* would love this one! He had an awkward moment of debating whether to join his family at the hospital or video this scenario. I'm proud to report, he went for the video camera. . . . Not really. He separated the two animals and came to join us.

Once Devin was stitched, we returned home for the rest of a day I thought would never end. You see, before my tranquil moment on the sofa, I had begun a cleaning project. It was the boys' room. You know the kind . . . where you dump all the drawers inside out, everything comes out of the closet, the mattresses are turned on end, and you are appalled at what is growing under the bed! Got the picture? This is the condition in which we left the house and the condition it was still in when we returned less than an hour before our dinner company was to arrive.

You must know our dinner guests were coming to see for themselves how homeschoolers really live! Well, they got an eyeful! Fortunately, they were polite guests, and given the circumstances of the day, they chose not to stay long.

Our guests had just pulled away when Devin came from his room, sobbing. I thought he had hit his head or broken his stitches, he was so hysterical. Until now, he hadn't shed a tear. Our greatest difficulty in the hospital was holding his head still. He was so busy inquiring about all the objects in the emergency room, the doctor was having trouble stitching straight.

Through the tears, he finally choked out, "My . . . only . . . gold . . . fish . . . die . . .d!" Whew! For a minute I thought it was something serious! We all assembled in the hall bathroom and dropped the goldfish into the commode. We stood silently for a moment, considering this loss. The next thing we knew the goldfish was swimming. We are now talking about a resurrected goldfish! True to his species this fish began swimming upstream. My husband got his hand stuck retrieving the goldfish, with our boys rooting him on. This was more than I could take! I didn't stay to watch him nearly stand on his head while the boys helped him twist his arm to get it loose. Nor did I assist in cleaning the fish tank for its homecoming. I called for every member of my family to be in bed and silent immediately, fish included!

While tucking my son in, I finally learned what had happened. Our swing set was sitting on our patio due to newly planted lawn. Devin, five years of age at the time, had tied himself to the top of the set and was attempting to fly. When the rope came loose, he landed on his head on a shovel on the concrete patio. The "play by play" made me shiver.

As a good teacher, I know to look for a teaching moment in every situation. I asked my son, "Honey, what did you learn from this experience, today?"

He looked sweetly into my eyes and replied so sincerely, "Mommy, I should have tied the rope tighter."

I collapsed into bed that night convinced I was not fit to homeschool, or for that matter for motherhood. Public school was not an option for our family, but a good boarding school was appealing. In this moment I was convinced that I and my family were failures.

Contrast this with another day. On this day I was running a few errands *alone*. If you have children, and I have a feeling you do or you wouldn't be interested in this book, you know how rare and how special these times can be.

The sky was blue, the air crisp and clean, the clouds fluffy, and the birds chirping as I pulled out of my driveway. I bought myself a mocha, which I didn't have to share. At each stop, I found the exact item for which I was looking, in the perfect color, size, style, on sale, etc. My husband and children had encouraged me to have this time to myself, and I felt so blessed.

While driving down the frontage road, a song came on the Christian radio station. The words caught my attention. "Life is precious, Life is sweet . . ."

Life is precious, I thought. *My life is sweet*! My husband is a dear, my children are adorable, and my life is peaches and cream! In this moment I was convinced that my family and I were a tremendous success.

Are you getting the picture? The reason I share these experiences with you is to help you see how easily we are swayed by our circumstances. We are emotional creatures and our emotions swing on the pendulum of life. In the two days I have described, my emotions dictated my perceptions of success and failure. This is a dangerous way to evaluate our lives and our children.

The purpose of this book is to help you take the emotion out of the way you evaluate the progress you and your children are making in each area of their education. It is designed to assist you in developing tools that make your assessments more objective. When we can separate one tough day away from the whole, we are more likely to carry on. When we can keep one delightful day in perspective, we are more inclined to remain consistent.

I am thankful that I did not throw in the towel on the marathon day I described earlier. I am equally as thankful that I did not boast to very many people of my family's infinite perfection on the second day. The same is true of any area of academic or character training. We all have ups and downs. The question is, "Are we continuing to move closer to the goal?" "What is the goal?" you ask. These pages ought to help you sort that out. In the meantime, give prayerful consideration to these suggestions. I pray they will help to steady your swing on the emotional pendulum and enable you to truly enjoy this precious time to learn and grow with your children. It is all too fleeting!

Model for Teaching & Evaluating

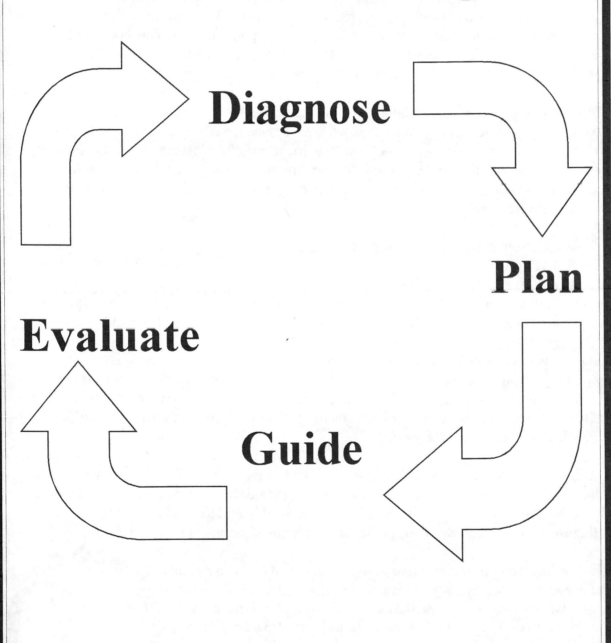

Diagnose

Plan

Guide

Evaluate

A MODEL FOR TEACHING AND EVALUATING

When, what, where, why, and how do we evaluate our children's progress? The answer is certainly always, in everything, everywhere, for every possible reason, through all of our senses, and then some. We are constantly concluding whether our children are "getting it," whether "it" is multiplication facts, the presidents in chronological order, the state capitals, or potty training. This book describes several tools to assist you in taking a look at where your students are now, but before looking at them, let's take a look at why we even bother with this process.

The tools described in this handbook are much like a road map. It is difficult, in fact very likely impossible, to discover how to reach your destination if you do not first determine where you *are*. Consequently, the first step for successful teaching and evaluation of student progress is determining where they *are*. In this first step we take a critical look at our students' skill and ability levels in order to **diagnose** their needs. We ask the question, "Where *are* we now?"

The second step in this model is to **plan** or set goals. Now the question becomes, "Where do we need or *want to be*?" Once we know where we *are*, we can more readily plan where we *want to be* and design a plan for getting there. In this step we decide it is time to master basic addition facts, read with fluency and expression, write descriptively, run the mile, respond quickly and cheerfully when called, or achieve other such goals we might set.

Thirdly, we must **guide** our students toward the goals that have been set. Webster says to guide is to "lead or direct in a way; to conduct in a course or path; to direct or order; to influence; to give direction to; to instruct; to regulate and manage." We need to direct the actions of our students so they will stay on the path toward the next goal. The question in the third step is, "What will we *do*?"

Finally, we **evaluate** our progress. Now we ask ourselves, "How *did* we *do*?" Are we any closer to our goals than we were when we diagnosed our current need? How much progress have we made? Is what we're doing working? This leads us back to a new **diagnosis** from which we **plan, guide,** and **evaluate** all over again.

It is so important to follow these steps in order. Too often, as parents and educators we attempt to evaluate student achievement when we have no idea where we started. Worse still, we use arbitrary assessment tools that don't accurately measure progress in the areas on which we have been working.

For example, we may go into a school year using a typical course of study: math, reading, writing, history, science, etc. In the spring we administer a standardized achievement test. If we have not taken the time to **diagnose** where we were in the fall, we have no idea if we have made any progress or not. This is exasperating to educators and students alike. Furthermore, without a clear plan to **plan** where we want to be and **guide** us to reach those goals, we don't even know what we are evaluating when we subject our students to hours of rigorous testing! We have just used someone else's method of **evaluation** to assess *our* student's achievement. That test might be useless in assessing our child's educational progress. The educational goals we've worked toward might differ dramatically from those evaluated by the standardized test.

If, on the other hand, we will first **diagnose** where our students are, **plan** goals based on their needs, and **guide** them with a course of study that addresses their needs, we can usually **evaluate** whether or not we are making progress on our own.

Consider your latest potty training experience. Did you need an expert to tell you your child needed to learn to control his bladder, and how and where it was appropriate for it to be emptied? Once you decided you were in the process of potty training, did you require an expert to determine whether you were succeeding? Of course not! Why not? Because when *you* set the goal, *you* know whether or not you are getting there. The same principles apply to every other area of the total education package. When *you* (parent/educator) determine where you *are* and where you need *to be*, *you* can decide if you are making progress or not.

The tools described in this book are just that, tools. They are not intended to control your teaching and learning experience. They are designed to help *you* take control of the education of your students and maintain it. As you look at evaluating student progress in this light, you will find it can actually be fun, even exciting, because it tells you something meaningful. It shows you where you are on the map, and you can plan your own destination! You can keep circling the block or you can plan an enterprising adventure! Don't wait around for the experts anymore. Determine today that you will **diagnose, plan, guide,** and **evaluate** your way to an exciting destination for yourself and your students!

Author's Note: I realize that the parents, teachers, and students who are using the materials in this book are both male and female. While it is not my intent to discriminate in any way, the pronoun "he" is used to refer to both genders for the sake of convention and simplicity.

DIAGNOSE

...to identify

"Where are we now?"

di-ag-nose´:
...to identify

"Where are we now?"

It is wise to take the time on a regular basis to use those materials and methods that help *you* diagnose *your* student's areas of mastery and needs in every curricular area in which you intend to see progress. The scope and sequence, checklists, and other forms in this section are offered as examples of diagnostic tools and are by no means exhaustive. Use them as a starting point to help you discover where you *are* in every area of the curriculum.

We expect that you will want to use some of the sample tools shown in each section, so the appendix includes reproducible originals that you are free to use for your own family.

Prepare to Progress...
DIAGNOSE

In order to be able to evaluate student progress at some appointed time in the future, it is necessary to know where the student *is* at the present. It is helpful to discover that a student has memorized his multiplication facts or that he can write a perfect paragraph. However, if he had mastered these skills a year ago, this would say something even more significant about progress. Unless we see additional skills displayed, there hasn't been much progress. Methods of determining where a student *is* at a given point in time in a given subject or skill area are considered *diagnostic*. Many diagnostic tools are available to today's parents and educators.

Observation

Simply watching your student work, or listening to him read can tell you much about his skills and level of ability. This is probably the most important tool to use with young children. You can record your observations on the "Observation Notes" pages provided in the appendix or create your own observation notebook.

Discussion

Engaging your student in a discussion can give you a good idea of his acquaintance with the material or subject matter. If a student can carry the conversation, he is probably familiar with the subject area. Our students will usually let us know what they think their skills are if we give them the opportunity. Very often they are right. Depending upon their maturity, you may continue discussing what they need to learn or what skills need to be improved upon next. "Observation Notes" can also be used to record your discussion concerning each of these academic areas. This allows you to spend special sharing time with your older students. You could simply ask your student to respond in writing, but the real value of this tool is in the discussion.

Interview

This is different from discussion in that you, the parent/teacher, are directing the conversation, primarily by asking questions. The student's answers will demonstrate his familiarity with the material or his ability to employ the skill or skills with which you are concerned.

Pre-Test

You can create your own to pre-test to find out how your student performs certain skills. However, many courses have pre- and post-tests built in for diagnostic purposes. Very often, the same test can be used to measure student progress after some teaching has taken place. Be certain students understand the purpose of a pre-test so they are not discouraged if they do poorly.

Diagnostic Tests

These are broad-based tests used to measure a student's skill level and compare it to other students the same age. They are standardized and are generally norm-referenced. One example of a diagnostic test is the Wide Range Achievement Test (WRAT), a broad screen of basic skills appropriate for nearly all ages that provides norm-referenced results. (Norm-referenced simply means a group of individuals have determined what is "normal" by comparing students of the same or similar ages and grade levels based on their performance on a particular test.) Generally, such tests must be administered by qualified individuals. However, there are a few that can be parent-administered.

Portfolio Sample

This is especially helpful in areas such as penmanship, writing skills, and art. This tool is much like a photograph of their abilities. It allows comparison of before and after examples that can be placed side-by-side to critique progress. Audio or video tapes can be useful in diagnosing with this method as well. See the section on "Creating a Portfolio" for more information on using portfolios for diagnosis and evaluation.

Inventory

An inventory is exactly what it sounds like. Before grocery shopping, take an inventory of your kitchen to be sure you stock up on the items your family likes to eat, cooking essentials and cleaning supplies. It's not fun to come home from the grocery store and realize you have three bottles of bleach and no laundry detergent. Before you go clothes shopping, you probably take an inventory of the closets to determine what fits, what's worn out, and what matches. You don't want to waste a trip or pass up a great sale on something you could really use.

The same applies to your educational inventory. By taking an inventory you can determine what you already have plenty of and in what items, skills and resources you need to invest time and money. It is prudent to take an inventory of every aspect of your educational program. You can design your own much like you create a shopping list. Simply write down what you believe your needs are. Then use your list to help you "shop" for ways to meet those needs. The "Student Inventory," as well as the "Reading Inventory" and "Writing Inventory" are provided to help you take inventory of your children's educational development. They are also included as suggestions for involving your student, however young, in the diagnostic process. The way he views his skills or abilities with regard to a particular subject area tells you alot about what his needs are.

Scope and Sequence

Sometimes we don't know what we should be looking for or which skills to expect our children to have acquired. A scope and sequence shows what skills are typically covered in various subject areas at different grade levels. "Scope" tells us how broad the coverage is; "sequence" tells us in what order skills should be mastered. There is no single scope and sequence that every child must follow. If we examine those from three or four sources (e.g., Bob Jones University Press, A Beka, Rod and Staff, our local school district), we will spot significant differences. This should reassure us of our right to make scope and sequence decisions of our own that are appropriate for our children. In this book, I have included the scope and sequence from the *Christian Home Education Curriculum Manual: Elementary Grades* for reading, grammar and composition, and mathematics for easy reference. However, you might want to request others from publishers or purchase more detailed versions such as those listed below:

Learning Objectives for Grades One Through Eight
Hewitt Educational Resources
P.O. Box 9
Washougal, WA 98671
(360) 835-8708

The Basic Skills Book
Creative Home Teaching
4721 Wendell St.
San Diego, CA 92105
(619) 263-8633

Skills Evaluation for the Home School
300 N. McKemy Ave.
Chandler, AZ 85226
(480) 438-2717 or (888) 367-9871 orders only

What Your Child Needs to Know
Family Christian Press
487 Myatt Dr.
Madison, TN 37115
(615) 860-3000

The tools provided in this section are designed to assist you in taking a closer look at where you *are* now. How the student compares with his peers is not nearly as important as how he progresses toward the goals you have for him and those he sets for himself. Therefore, diagnostic tools should be selected because they help you determine which skills and abilities are mastered and which need continued reinforcement—not because they provide a comparison such as a percentile ranking.

Keep in mind that anything that helps you determine where you and your students *are* is a diagnostic tool. The examples that follow are only a few of the tools you might use for diagnosing.

EDUCATOR'S OBJECTIVES

While we're identifying our children's educational needs, it's worth taking a few minutes to address our own. There is a saying often used in motivation and sales seminars: "The formula for perpetual ignorance is this: Be content with your own knowledge and satisfied with your own opinions." I believe it also applies to us as parents.

As educators we must continue to grow and learn, or the well out of which we give and teach will run dry. On the "Educator's Objectives" form, list the areas in which you would like to see growth in yourself as an educator in the coming year. Describe how you intend to accomplish each objective so you will be better equipped to guide your students toward the goals you have for them.

Keep in mind the variety of resources available to you:
- Books
- Audio and video tapes
- Seminars, conventions, workshops
- Educational magazines and other literature
- People with an expertise in the areas in which you need help
- More experienced colleagues
- Support groups and independent study programs
- Home School Legal Defense Association
- Curriculum Fairs

You will probably think of additional resources. Keep your eyes and ears open. Just as we look for "teachable moments" for our children, there are many learning and growing opportunities available to us if we are also "teachable."

The "Educator's Diagnostic Survey" on the following page might help you determine some of your strengths and weaknesses with regard to your home schooling program. Once you have completed this form, begin with the areas in which you feel least competent (those with the lowest number on a scale of 0 to 10) to set objectives for yourself. Consider using the "Educator's Objectives" form (p. 155) to help you with this.

The more *you* learn the more you will enthusiastically motivate your students and yourself to a lifetime of learning!

Educator's Diagnostic Survey

Area of personal skill or ability in teaching my children	Evaluate on a scale of 0 - 10 0=no ability/experience 10=mastered
Confidence about teaching my children at home	0 1 2 3 4 5 6 7 8 9 10
Developing a clear philosophy and purpose for my educational program	0 1 2 3 4 5 6 7 8 9 10
Organizing the schooling environment	0 1 2 3 4 5 6 7 8 9 10
Managing my home so I can teach	0 1 2 3 4 5 6 7 8 9 10
Planning ahead	0 1 2 3 4 5 6 7 8 9 10
Planning overall curriculum	0 1 2 3 4 5 6 7 8 9 10
Teaching and evaluating Bible	0 1 2 3 4 5 6 7 8 9 10
Teaching and evaluating reading	0 1 2 3 4 5 6 7 8 9 10
Teaching and evaluating writing	0 1 2 3 4 5 6 7 8 9 10
Teaching and evaluating history (geography, social studies, government, etc.)	0 1 2 3 4 5 6 7 8 9 10
Teaching and evaluating health and sciences	0 1 2 3 4 5 6 7 8 9 10
Teaching and evaluating the arts	0 1 2 3 4 5 6 7 8 9 10
Teaching and evaluating physical education	0 1 2 3 4 5 6 7 8 9 10
Teaching several grade levels at a time (if applicable)	0 1 2 3 4 5 6 7 8 9 10
Disciplining myself to complete school work	0 1 2 3 4 5 6 7 8 9 10
Disciplining my children to complete school work	0 1 2 3 4 5 6 7 8 9 10

master form in appendix *SAMPLE*

Meeting each child's individual needs

Setting goals and objectives

Finding enjoyment in home schooling

Knowing my state requirements for my home-schooling program

Being informed and aware of current issues that could affect my home schooling program

Creating and following a school schedule

Planning special activities (ie., field trips, cooperative study classes, library, etc.)

> You might use this as a starting place for yourself and set a goal to retake this survey at regular intervals. For example, each time you are diagnosing your children's skills, you might use this to see how you are growing as well. Some will find it easier to diagnose their own progress at separate times in order to concentrate more fully. Do whatever works for you, but remember the best way to lead your children toward a lifetime of learning is by example!

Suggested Scope and Sequence

The following learning goals are offered to assist you in setting goals and guiding your students toward them. While the list is not comprehensive, it does give you an idea of the different types of skills you will likely want to incorporate into each grade level. Remember, grade level is determined by your diagnosis of your children's needs and readiness and not by age.

Learning Goals for Reading Skills

The following learning goals are not categorized by grade level, but are listed in general in order of developmental ability. They can be used with pre-readers through high school level.

- [ ] Recognize consonant letter sounds
- [ ] Recognize vowel sounds (short vowels before long)
- [ ] Know letter names
- [ ] Recognize upper and lower case letters
- [ ] Recognize that sounds make up words
- [ ] Distinguish like and unlike sounds
- [ ] Retell a story that was read to him
- [ ] Use left to right sequence when reading
- [ ] Follow simple oral directions
- [ ] Blend sounds together
- [ ] Make simple words with movable alphabet
- [ ] Dramatize a reading selection that is read to him
- [ ] Read aloud simple words
- [ ] Identify public and safety signs
- [ ] Recognize name, address, phone number
- [ ] Recognize patterns
- [ ] Recognize blends, digraphs, and diphthongs
- [ ] Recognize basic sight words
- [ ] Recognize root words
- [ ] Begin to recognize suffixes
- [ ] Read aloud, including "oral punctuation" (e.g., stopping at ends of sentences and raising the voice for questions.)
- [ ] Use a primary picture dictionary
- [ ] Use context clues to decode words
- [ ] Use context clues to help predict
- [ ] Retell a story (that has been read silently or aloud) with the proper sequence of events
- [ ] Identify the main idea
- [ ] Recognize and form compound words
- [ ] Recognize the number of syllables in words
- [ ] Understand and apply phonics skills consistently
- [ ] Read basic sight vocabulary
- [ ] Arrange words in alphabetical order by second letter
- [ ] Draw conclusions from a given set of facts
- [ ] Read to find answers to specific questions
- [ ] Recognize contractions
- [ ] Read and recognize common prefixes and suffixes
- [ ] Recognize homonyms, synonyms, and antonyms

- [ ] Recognize words and phrases that tell who, what, when, where, why, or how
- [ ] Predict story information
- [ ] Predict story sequence
- [ ] Identify two or more syllables in words
- [ ] Retell a story after reading it alone
- [ ] Dramatize an individual reading selection
- [ ] Follow written directions
- [ ] Read for pleasure
- [ ] Read grade-level material with fluency
- [ ] Identify the moral of the story
- [ ] Use a table of contents
- [ ] Use a glossary
- [ ] Use guide words to locate words in dictionary
- [ ] Locate title, author, and illustrator
- [ ] Read for meaning
- [ ] Draw conclusions
- [ ] Identify main and supporting characters
- [ ] Identify supporting details
- [ ] Recognize or infer cause and effect
- [ ] Differentiate between reality and fantasy
- [ ] Differentiate between fact and opinion
- [ ] Participate in choral reading
- [ ] Develop new vocabulary
- [ ] Read whole sections of text as opposed to word by word
- [ ] Understand prefixes and suffixes on more difficult levels (e.g., study of Greek and Latin influences)
- [ ] Read aloud with increasing skill and expression
- [ ] Use reading skills to locate information
- [ ] Follow more difficult written directions
- [ ] Listen to adult reading and participate in discussion
- [ ] Use a dictionary to discover the meaning and pronunciation of words
- [ ] Develop proofreading skills
- [ ] Practical reading skills: newspaper, advertisements, schedules, etc.
- [ ] Use a variety of reference materials for locating information
- [ ] Use different parts of a book to acquire information
- [ ] Use on-line information services, CD-ROMs, and other electronic reference materials
- [ ] Read, interpret, and draw conclusions from

charts, graphs, schedules, diagrams
- ☐ Skim/scan material to find information appropriate to use in an outline
- ☐ Identify author's point of view
- ☐ Read materials for literary value
- ☐ Identify setting, plot, conflict, theme, and style in literature
- ☐ Compare and contrast elements contained in reading material
- ☐ Describe and draw inferences about characters in literature
- ☐ Read and study a variety of forms of prose and poetry
- ☐ Identify and interpret various forms of figurative language including similes and metaphors
- ☐ Analyze reading materials for technique, personal appeal, effectiveness
- ☐ Become familiar with some renowned authors and their works
- ☐ Compare authors and their works

Learning Goals for Composition and Grammar

The following learning goals are taken from the <u>*Christian Home Educators' Curriculum Manual:*</u> <u>*Elementary Grades*</u> *by Cathy Duffy.*

Approximately first-grade level
- ☐ Speak in complete sentences
- ☐ Follow oral directions
- ☐ Tell short stories
- ☐ Say name, address, phone number
- ☐ Recognize rhymes
- ☐ Listen to others reading
- ☐ Relate simple stories, verses, or rhymes orally
- ☐ Write simple sentences ending with periods
- ☐ Capitalize first letters of sentences, proper names, the pronoun "I"

Approximately second-grade level
- ☐ Follow oral instructions
- ☐ Add suffixes s, ed, and ing
- ☐ Recognize some uses of apostrophes
- ☐ Alphabetize by first letter
- ☐ Follow series of instructions
- ☐ Introduce syllables
- ☐ Use simple dictionary
- ☐ Write original short stories, notes, reports
- ☐ Capitalize days, months, cities, streets, states, references to God and the Bible

Approximately third-grade level
- ☐ Follow oral directions
- ☐ Write and relate original stories, reports, etc.
- ☐ Use simple punctuation

- ☐ Recognize and use complete sentences
- ☐ Capitalize initials
- ☐ Use some prefixes and suffixes
- ☐ Follow logical sequence in telling or writing stories, reports, etc.
- ☐ Use dictionary
- ☐ Alphabetize
- ☐ Recognize number of syllables in words

Approximately fourth-grade level
- ☐ (Note: Grammar becomes a more important aspect of language arts as children learn proper word usage to improve their writing skills.)
- ☐ Participate in discussion
- ☐ Write simple stories, poems, letters, reports, etc.
- ☐ Simple punctuation used correctly: period, comma, exclamation point, and question mark
- ☐ Use periods after abbreviations and initials
- ☐ Use commas properly in word series, dates, greetings and closings of letters
- ☐ Use apostrophes in some contractions and in possessive words
- ☐ Group related sentences to form a paragraph
- ☐ Write simple letter and address envelope
- ☐ Identify nouns and verbs
- ☐ Improve dictionary skills
- ☐ Use correct verb forms–singular/plurals, present, past, future

Approximately fifth-grade level
(Note: In most programs, grammar and other concepts are repeated at increasing levels of difficulty each year. The emphasis shifts to writing and vocabulary skills since phonics and foundational language skills should have been mastered by this level.)
- ☐ Interpret oral information
- ☐ Judge content and presentation
- ☐ Participate in discussions
- ☐ Give oral reports
- ☐ Use punctuation correctly including quotation marks around titles and direct quotations
- ☐ Underline titles
- ☐ Write notes, invitations, book reports, original prose and poetry
- ☐ Proofread and edit one's own written work
- ☐ Identify nouns, verbs, adjectives, adverbs, pronouns
- ☐ Identify prepositions, conjunctions, interjections
- ☐ Identify subjects, predicates, direct objects
- ☐ Recognize subject-predicate agreement
- ☐ Use adjectives and adverbs in writing
- ☐ Use verbs correctly

☐ Identify prepositions, conjunctions, interjections

☐ Recognize agreement between pronouns and antecedents

☐ Recognize irregular plurals

☐ Diagram subjects and predicates*

☐ Diagram direct objects*

☐ Diagram adjectives and adverbs*

☐ Diagram prepositions and conjunctions*

☐ Recognize indirect objects*

☐ Diagram indirect objects*

Approximately sixth through eighth-grade levels
(Note: Goals will vary greatly according to each student's progress. We include goals through eighth grade so you can better plan a long-range schedule of when to accomplish which goals.)

☐ Give oral reports

☐ Participate in discussions

☐ Use plural possessives and contractions

☐ Recognize and write compound sentences

☐ Identify and write topic sentences

☐ Write outlines

☐ Write using correct punctuation including quotation marks, indentation, colons, and semicolons

☐ Write compositions, dialogue, simple poetry, short research papers, book reports

☐ Write business and friendly letters

☐ Write with unity and coherence

☐ Proofread and edit one's own work

☐ Use dictionary to locate word origins, dictionary spellings (pronunciations), usage

☐ Recognize appositives and direct address

☐ Recognize helping and linking verbs

☐ Identify predicate adjective and predicate nominative (noun)

☐ Recognize and diagram basic parts of speech: subject, verb, adjectives, adverbs, prepositions, conjunctions*

☐ Diagram more complicated sentences*

☐ Recognize prepositional phrases

☐ Diagram predicate nominative and predicate adjective*

☐ Do oral presentation dramatically

☐ Understand use of italics

☐ Recognize and use simple similes and metaphors

☐ Use thesaurus

☐ Take notes from printed and oral material

☐ Know how to use card catalog or library cataloging system and other reference materials

☐ Organize information from reference materials for reports

☐ Write research paper including brief bibliography (seventh-eighth grade)

☐ Apply proper word usage in writing and speech
*Instead of diagramming you might use *Winston Grammar* (Precious Memories Educational Resources) or Montessori methods for identifying parts of speech.

Mathematics Concepts & Goals

Concepts are listed in an approximate sequence which builds skill upon skill. Grade levels are also approximations.

Kindergarten level

☐ Comparison: same/different; larger/smaller; shorter/taller; long, longer, longest.

☐ Classification: by color, shape, size, common characteristic

☐ Correspondence: matching items one for one, recognizing like amounts

☐ Duplicate or extend given pattern by color or shape

☐ Identify four basic shapes—circle, square, rectangle, triangle

☐ Recognize numbers 0 - 10

☐ Count and print numbers 0 - 10

☐ Identify more/less-larger/smaller of numbers 0 - 10

☐ Compare numbers of objects

☐ Perform pictorial addition 0 - 10

☐ Name coins: penny, nickel, dime

Approximately first-grade level

☐ Count backwards from 10 - 0

☐ Addition with numbers 0 - 10

☐ Match set with numbers 0 - 20

☐ Subtraction with numbers 0 - 10

☐ Subtraction with numbers 0 - 20

☐ Count, read, write numbers to 100

☐ Recognize smaller/larger numbers to 100

☐ Count backwards from 20 - 0

☐ Recall addition facts to 10

☐ Recognize that $2 + 4$ is the same as $4 + 2$ (commutative property)

☐ Recognize addition and subtraction in various formats–horizontal and vertical.

☐ Recall subtraction facts for numbers 10 or less

☐ Recognize quarters (money)

☐ Count coins to $.25

☐ Recognize time to the hour and half hour

☐ Recognize fraction shapes 1/2 and 1/4

☐ Count by 10s to 100

☐ Represent two-digit numbers in place value form as tens and ones

- ☐ Read, write, and use expanded notation (e.g., 60 + 9 for 69)
- ☐ Perform two-digit addition and subtraction without carrying
- ☐ Read calendar
- ☐ Select correct operation for problem solving (i.e., addition/subtraction)
- ☐ Think about practical application of arithmetic
- ☐ Identify and continue simple patterns
- ☐ Select, collect, record, or organize data using tallies, charts, graphs, and tables

Approximately second-grade level

- ☐ Use symbols for "greater than" and "less than"
- ☐ Count by 2s and 5s to 100
- ☐ Represent three-digit numbers in place value form as hundreds, tens, and ones
- ☐ Read and write three-digit numbers
- ☐ Select largest or smallest of numbers to 999
- ☐ Recall addition and subtraction facts to 9 + 9 (some children will need a delay before mastering subtraction)
- ☐ Two-digit addition with carrying (regrouping)
- ☐ Two-digit subtraction with borrowing (regrouping)
- ☐ Introduce multiplication concept
- ☐ Represent simple multiplication concepts with numbers
- ☐ Identify halves, thirds, fourths
- ☐ Know value of penny, nickel, dime, quarter, etc.
- ☐ Count coins to $1.00
- ☐ Recognize time to quarter hour
- ☐ Simple measurement: linear, liquid, weight
- ☐ Interpret bar graph
- ☐ Solve one-step word problem with addition or subtraction

Approximately third-grade level

- ☐ Do multiplication to 9 x 9 = 81 (Note: Mastery of times tables may not occur until fourth or fifth grade.)
- ☐ Introduce division concept pictorially or with hands-on materials
- ☐ Identify plane value in four and five-digit numbers
- ☐ Read and write up to five-digit numbers
- ☐ Recognize odd and even numbers
- ☐ Do three-digit additions and subtractions with regrouping (carrying/borrowing)
- ☐ Identify missing function (+,-,x,÷)
- ☐ Identify and complete more difficult patterns/sequences
- ☐ Recognize 1/2, 1/3, and 1/4 of different objects
- ☐ Read and write time to nearest five minutes
- ☐ Understand a.m. and p.m.

- ☐ Read calendar, know days of week, and names of months
- ☐ Count, add, subtract money using dollar sign and decimal point
- ☐ Measure length, capacity (liquid measure), and mass (weight) using both English and metric measurements
- ☐ Interpret line and bar graphs
- ☐ Identify patterns and relationships from organized data; draw conclusions
- ☐ Solve one-step word problems using addition, subtraction, multiplication, division
- ☐ Do mental computation
- ☐ Recognize reasonable and unreasonable estimates in simple problem solving
- ☐ Make up word problems from given data
- ☐ Interpret and make up codes

Approximately fourth-grade level

- ☐ Identify place value in digits up to seven numbers
- ☐ Read and write numbers with seven digits
- ☐ Do addition and subtraction with whole numbers
- ☐ Do two-digit subtraction with whole numbers
- ☐ Do two-digit times three-digit multiplication
- ☐ Round off numbers and estimate multiplication and division answers
- ☐ Divide with two-digit divisors
- ☐ Show remainders in division as whole numbers and fractions
- ☐ Introduce addition of fractions with like denominators
- ☐ Understand fractions as ratios
- ☐ Addition and subtraction of fractions with like denominators
- ☐ Recognize and create equivalent fractions
- ☐ Define, identify, and use factors, multiples, greatest common factors, least common multiples
- ☐ Simplify fractions (reducing to lowest terms)
- ☐ Identify fractions on number line
- ☐ Read and write time to nearest minute
- ☐ Do all operations with money; make change
- ☐ More difficult level of measurement: length, capacity, mass
- ☐ Determine perimeter of any polygon
- ☐ Familiarity: lines, segments, cubes, pyramids
- ☐ Construct bar graph
- ☐ Add/subtract mixed numbers
- ☐ Multiply and divide fractions
- ☐ Identify and complete more complicated patterns
- ☐ Solve two-step word problems

- ☐ Use data to construct word problems
- ☐ Determine missing data for problem solution
- ☐ Analyze problems
- ☐ Define and find averages

Approximately fifth-grade level

- ☐ Determine prime factors
- ☐ Read and write up to nine-digit numbers
- ☐ Introduce decimals to thousandths
- ☐ Do any addition, subtraction, multiplication, division problems with whole numbers
- ☐ Add, subtract, and multiply any decimals
- ☐ Divide whole numbers by decimals
- ☐ Express division remainders as decimals
- ☐ Use ratio
- ☐ More difficult measurements
- ☐ Determine area of rectangles and squares
- ☐ Introduce concept of volume with cubes
- ☐ Round whole numbers or decimals
- ☐ Accurately estimate answers
- ☐ Recognize congruence and symmetry
- ☐ Become familiar with diameter and radius of circle; angles; and parallel, perpendicular, and intersecting lines (define and draw)
- ☐ Construct and interpret line graphs
- ☐ Compute area of triangle
- ☐ Apply math skills to life situations
- ☐ Perform mental computation
- ☐ Apply logical thinking to problems and life situations

Approximately sixth-grade level

- ☐ Read and write numbers up to twelve digits
- ☐ Read and write all decimals
- ☐ Understand and use terminating and repeating decimals
- ☐ Do any computation with fractions and decimals
- ☐ Convert fractions to decimals and decimals to fractions
- ☐ Determine circumference and area of circles
- ☐ Use protractor to measure and draw angles
- ☐ Measure and make triangles (include some that are not equilateral)
- ☐ Interpret circle graphs
- ☐ Convert measures from one type of unit to another within the same system
- ☐ Formulate and apply problem -solving strategy (application of logic)
- ☐ Change percents to decimals
- ☐ Understand and apply percentage
- ☐ Introduce integers
- ☐ Introduce exponential notation
- ☐ Define, explain, and use probability
- ☐ Analyze and evaluate statistics

Many tools included here are multipurpose in nature. For example, the scope and sequence could be used to diagnose skills that need to be addressed, to plan goals, to guide the student through a course of study, and again, to evaluate progress made. In this way the scope and sequence not only helps you to identify which skills you expect your student to master at this level, but which you will need help in addressing. You might feel capable of teaching all of the kindergarten math skills and concepts without purchasing a math text or any other materials. However, you may look at fourth or sixth grade in a different light. It could be that you feel you can address all but a few of the third grade grammar and composition skills using the scope and sequence as a checklist for mastery. In this case, you will look for resources that fill in the gaps instead of buying an entire grammar text simply because it's the right "grade level."

Likewise, a number of the other tools you find in this book will accomplish the same purpose. It can often be helpful to use the same checklist or critique to diagnose and to evaluate. This serves as a pre- and post-test. Consider using the "Diagnostic Reading" and "Diagnostic Writing Checklists." These can help you determine your student's specific areas of need and readiness as well as to plan goals. It will further assist you in selecting instructional materials that specifically target or emphasize the areas of need. In the long run, this approach can save you time and money!

Diagnostic Reading Checklist

Student Name *Devin*   Date *9 - 7 - 99*

Reading Process	Frequently	Occasionally	Comments
Word Identification Strategies			
I. Reading Intention: Reads for meaning (comprehension)	✓		
II. Predicting: Uses context clues to predict	✓		
Rejects unsatisfactory predictions	✓		
Integrates meaning	✓		
III. Attention: Able to take whole sections of text (in contrast to word by word reading)		✓	
Omits words in text			*seldom*
Transposes words in text		✓	
Adds words in text		✓	

Substitutes words for words that:
    Look similar
    Have similar meaning
    Sound similar
    Change meaning
		✓
		✓
		✓
		✓	

IV. When In Difficulty: Reads on to the end of a sentence	✓		
Rereads sentence	✓		
Uses initial letters as clues		✓	
Uses pictorial clues		✓	
Waits for help	✓	✓	
Quits			*much better...rarely*

SAMPLE

21

Reading Process	Frequently	Occasionally	Comments
V. Reading Newer/Longer Words :			
Selects cues	✓		
Blends word parts	✓		
VI. Monitoring:			
Self-corrects	✓ *usually*		
READING PRODUCT:			
Comprehension	✓		
VII. Prediction:			
Predicts story information	✓		
Predicts story sequence (what might happen...)	✓		
VIII. Analyzing/ Associating:			
Can retell story or information in own words	✓		*in great detail*
Can recognize or infer: Main idea	✓		
Details	✓		
Character development		✓	
Can recognize or infer: Sequence	✓		
Cause and effect		✓	
Comparison	✓		*difficult concept now*
Can make judgments of: Values		✓	
Reality and fantasy			*R/F, F/O not very well*
Fact and opinion			
Can appreciate an author's skill			*Not yet*

Student Reading Inventory

Name *Devin, age 8* **Date** *Dec. 1998*

My Reading

SAMPLE

Evaluate on a scale of 0 - 10
0=not very much   10=very much

I like to read.	0 1 2 3 4 5 (6) 7 8 9 10
I am a good reader.	0 1 2 3 4 5 6 7 (8) 9 10
I am a fast reader.	0 1 2 3 (4) 5 6 7 8 9 10
I understand what I read by myself.	0 1 2 3 4 5 (6) 7 8 9 10
I understand what someone else reads to me.	0 1 2 3 4 5 6 7 8 (9) 10
The things I read are interesting.	0 1 2 3 4 5 6 7 8 (9) 10
I have a lot of books.	0 1 2 3 4 5 6 7 8 9 (10)
I like to tell others about the things I read about.	0 1 2 3 4 5 (6) 7 8 9 10

My favorite book is ___*The Best Christmas Pageant Ever*___

My favorite author is ___*Dr. Seuss*___

My favorite type of reading material is ___*cartoons in the newspaper*___

My favorite time to read is ___*during afternoon quiet time*___

My favorite place to read is ___*on my bed or by the Christmas tree*___

My favorite thing to read about is ___*electricity*___

The last two books I read with someone else were ___*A Christmas Box,*___
   A Christmas Carol

The last two books I read by myself were ___*Rainy Day Cooking,*___
Poisonous Snakes

Something I would like to read more is ___*detective stories*___

Teacher Notes: *Devin told me his answers and I wrote them down. He seemed to enjoy thinking about his reading. It's interesting that he sees himself as a fairly good reader even though he doesn't think he's a very fast reader.*

Diagnostic Writing Checklist

Student Name __Kenny__   Date __9-05-99__

Writing Features	Frequently	Occasionally	Not Enough Information	Comments
I. Organizational Features:				
Sequence of ideas/details	✓			
Cause and effect	✓			
Transitions		✓		
Introductions (i.e. beginnings)		✓		
Conclusions (i.e. endings)		✓		
II. Developmental Features:				
Sentence sense		✓		
Story sense	✓			
Moral sense		✓		
Topic depth			✓	
Risk taking (Does the writer experiment, try new things?)			✓	
III. Sentence Features:				
Simple sentences	✓			
Compounding (combining sentences together)	✓			Sentences are combined, but are run-on
Variety: in beginnings		✓		
in endings		✓		
in length		✓		
Organization into paragraphs				not writing in paragraphs yet

SAMPLE

Writing Features	Frequently	Occasionally	Not Enough Information	Comments
IV. Stylistic Features:				
Literal language	✓			
Images				*No images, metaphors, comparisons or similes*
Metaphors				
Comparisons/similes				
Vivid vocabulary		✓		
Detailed descriptions		✓		
Sentence variety				*All start with 'the' or 'I'*
V. Mechanical Features:				
Punctuation				*not much*
Capitalization	*'I' and names*			
Possessives		✓		
Contractions		✓		
Subject-verb agreement		✓		
Tense agreement (past, present, future)				*frequently confuses*
Verb endings		✓		
Spelling (phonetic, conventional)	✓			

Student Writing Inventory

Name _Wendell, age 11_　　　　Date _Sept. 1999_

My Reading

SAMPLE

Evaluate on a scale of 0 - 10
0=not very much　10=very much

I like to write.　　　　　　　　　　0 1 2 3 4 5 (6) 7 8 9 10

I am a good writer.　　　　　　　　0 1 2 3 4 5 6 7 8 (9) 10

Writing is an important skill.　　　　0 1 2 3 4 5 6 7 8 9 (10)

I like to show my writing to others.　0 1 2 3 4 5 6 (7) 8 9 10

The things I write are interesting.　　0 1 2 3 (4) 5 6 7 8 9 10

Others can read and understand my writing.　0 1 2 3 4 5 (6) 7 8 9 10

I write a lot.　　　　　　　　　　　0 1 2 3 4 5 6 7 8 (9) 10

What I'm best at writing is _letters to friends_

I think writing is important because _it helps you get a job and you're more likely to keep your job_

The kind of writing I like to do most is _journaling and taking lecture notes_

My favorite time to write is _when it's raining and quiet_

My favorite place to write is _in the classroom by the window_

My favorite thing to write about is _my day_

The last writing I did was _a recipe for my grandma_

To become a better writer I need help with _my spelling_

Something I would like to write is _a book titled "Life With My Mom"_

Teacher Notes: _While Wendell enjoys writing, I'm surprised he doesn't feel his writing is interesting. We need to work on that._

Diagnosing Writing Skills

These writing directions are given as suggestions to assist you in prompting your student's writing. These writing situations might be used to diagnose your student's writing skills prior to teaching composition or mechanics. They might also be used at the end of a period of instruction to evaluate progress. Students should be encouraged to keep writing selections in a a portfolio. It would be wise to keep a pre-instruction writing sample for comparison with samples after the student has been working on specific skills.

Preparing for Prompting the Writing Sample
It is important to prepare your students for this writing situation, particularly if this is new for them. You need to make some decisions before you begin. What are you looking for in their writing? Will you be evaluating mechanics, content, use of descriptive vocabulary, spelling, organization of thoughts and ideas, etc.?

If your goal is to see what they are capable of on their own, make it clear that you will not be helping them with any part of this assignment. If you will help them with some part of their writing (e.g., spelling), make that clear. Many parents find that the less help they make available, the more resourceful their students become. It might be helpful to set a time limit as well.

Decide on a topic for the writing situation. You could use the same topic for all your budding writers or change the topic for older or younger students. You might consider using the same topic for all ages, with an explanation that you have different expectations for what they will accomplish.

Explain to your students what you plan to do with this assignment. It's been a long time since you mentioned diagnosing. If they are used to copying dictated letters to Grandma, they might become frustrated when you do not edit for them. Even if they are comfortable with original composition and write frequently, they might be used to having more time than you are allowing for this assignment. Be certain they understand that this writing sample will not be rewritten, polished, or improved at a later time, but should be their best effort within the time allowed.

You could write the topic on a chalk or dry erase board or directly on a paper so your student can refer to it. You might also consider leaving the room so you are not tempted to give too much help. Remember, what you want to know is how *he* puts ideas in writing.

Once you receive a writing sample from your student, use one of the tools for evaluating writing, such as the "Diagnostic Writing Checklist" in this section to assess his skills and decide what needs to be addressed for improvement and development.

Writing Prompts

Once you have prepared yourself and your students for the writing situation, give them one of the following topics or create one of your own. Older students might help you come up with topics that would be interesting for them. Following these prompts, a writing sample is laid out to give you an idea of how you might use it with your students.

🖉 Different families celebrate holidays differently. Which holiday do you like best? How does your family celebrate? Who do you celebrate it with and where? What activities and foods are part of your family's holiday tradition? What special meaning does it have for you? Write an essay describing your favorite holiday.

🖉 If you could dine with anyone in the world who would it be and why? Where would you go? What would you discuss? How would you prepare for dinner with this person? What would you wear? What would you eat? How would you get there? What difference would this dinner make in your life? Write an essay describing your dinner.

🖉 What character traits make a good friend? Do you have a friend who has these qualities? If not, why do you spend time with them? Which character traits are most important? Which ones would you sacrifice for others? Which ones make you a good friend to someone else? Write an essay describing what makes a good friend.

🖉 If you could be invisible for a day, what would you do? Where would you go? How would you get there? Would you try to let your parents know what happened to you? Would you do these same things if you were visible? Why or why not? Write a story about your invisible day.

🖉 Do you think boys or girls have it easier in life? Why do you think the way you do? Do you have specific evidence, people, or situations to support your ideas? Write an essay about who has it easier, boys or girls.

🖉 What would you do if everyone in your family forgot your birthday? Would you remind them? How? How would you feel? Would it cause you to treat others differently on their birthdays? Write a letter to your family describing your feelings and your response to their forgetting your birthday.

🖉 If this weekend you could do absolutely anything you wanted, what would you do? Where would you go? With whom would you spend your time? Have you spent a weekend this way in the past? Why or why not? Write an essay describing your perfect weekend.

🖉 Would you like to have an identical twin? What about it would be best? What would be worst? How do you think he or she would feel to have you for a twin? Write an essay describing what life would be like with an identical twin.

🖉 Which school subjects do you think will be important to you in the future? How will they affect your life? Are there any which you think will be useless? Why? Write an essay discussing how your current studies will affect your life in the future.

Writing Prompts

✎ Television has become controversial in many circles today. Do you think television is healthy for young people today? Why or why not? Can you list some positive uses for TV? What are the problems with TV today? Do the benefits outweigh the negative effects? How does TV affect you in your life? Does it influence people who don't watch it? How? Write an essay supporting your views of television.

✎ Would you rather be a rich and famous person or a great doctor who saves a lot of people but is not wealthy or well known? What would be the benefits of being in either situation? What would be the drawbacks? Do you think you will ever find yourself in either situation? Why? Write an essay describing your viewpoint.

✎ If you could be as talented at any one thing as someone you know, what would you choose? Why? How would your life be different if you had as much talent as this person? What would you do with it? Who else would your talent affect? Write an essay describing your life with your new talent?

✎ If you could take a round-trip ride in a time machine to anyplace in the past or future, where would you want to go? What time period would it be? Why would you go there? What do you think you would learn? Write an essay describing your experience.

✎ What does it mean to be "grown-up?" When do you think you will be "grown-up?" When do you think your parents will see you as a "grown-up?" Are you in a hurry to "grow up?" Why? Write an essay describing what it means to be "grown-up."

✎ One day your father gets a really weird idea and dyes his hair green. He asks you to go to the shopping center with him. Would you go? Why or why not? Would you be impressed or embarrassed? Why? What would your decision say to your father? Write a story about this situation and your response to it.

✎ What is a hero? Is it important to have heroes? Why or why not? Who are your heroes? Why are they so terrific? Do you think they should be your friends' heroes also? Write an essay describing heroes.

✎ Much literature has been written about people who were willing to die for great causes. Is there anything so important to you that you would be willing to give up your life for it? What is it? What makes it that important? What would it mean to you to give it up in your life? Write a letter to your family telling them why you would rather die than give up this important part of your life.

✎ People have differing philosophies of education. What is education? What makes a good education? How is it carried out? Who is involved in it? Are you receiving a good education? Why or why not? Write an essay describing education.

✎ Many issues make the news today. People have different views of which issues are important. What world issue is important to you? Why? How does it affect you? How does it affect the world today? What would you do about this issue if you were given the opportunity to make a change? Write an essay discussing the issue, its impact, and your solution.

Student Writing Sample

Name _____ Date _____

Writing Topic
Different families celebrate holidays differently. Which holiday do you like best? How does your family celebrate? Who do you celebrate it with and where? What activities and foods are part of your family's holiday tradition? What special meaning does it have for you?

Directions
Write an essay describing your favorite holiday. Use as many describing words as you can so the person reading your essay will understand why it is so special for you. Be sure to use correct punctuation, spelling, and grammar.

_____

_____

_____

_____

_____

_____

_____

_____

_____

_____

_____

_____

_____

_____

_____

_____

_____

_____

_____

_____

OBSERVATION NOTES

Keep this list in a convenient location and add to it throughout the day or week. Date each entry if they are not made on the same day. Anytime you make a "mental note," it should be added to your observation notes. Observe not just the finished product in each area but the attitude toward the subject, length of time needed to accomplish related tasks, mistakes which are repeatedly made, teacher and student likes and dislikes, how much time is devoted to the area of study, etc. This will help to fill in the gaps left by other diagnostic tools which are more academic in form and purpose.

SAMPLE

Character

Doesn't follow directions until given the 4th time. Impolite, seldom says please/thank-you when in public. Treated brother with consideration but impatient when I'm working with brother. Desires to be helpful whenever possible. Follows Dad's directions better than Mom's. Puts toys away well.

Reading
(Aloud and silent)

Enjoys reading aloud with Mom or Dad (also Grandma), in car, too. Short attention span for reading silently (approx. 5 min). Not decoding well. Relies on picture cues a lot. Frustrated when word doesn't come easily. Waits for help often. Picks up books frequently throughout day. Brings them to Mom to read. Generally seems to enjoy "easy" books.

Penmanship

Laborious, uneven, hard to read, "not fun," trouble sitting still when writing. Also has trouble holding onto pencil. Enjoys making cards & pictures, but not writing for "school."

OBSERVATION NOTES

Spelling

Phonetic spelling. Wants Mom to spell out any "new" words; doesn't rely on rules he has learned. Tries to ask brother if Mom doesn't spell for him. Enjoys "spell out" game at lowest level.

Writing

Enjoys writing cards & notes. Considers "school" writing "not fun." Writes about 3 lines before tiring out. Creative. Writing makes sense. Enjoys reading his writing back to Mom when he can read his penmanship.

Mathematics

Loves math! Likes to play math games. Thinks flash cards are fun. Likes to count money. Can add 2 digit numbers in head! Understands concept of x. Thinks workbook is boring.

Science

Loves zoobooks, and wildlife encyclopedias! Enjoys looking for bugs and collecting leaves & flowers (especially neighbors)! Likes ICR dinosaur books. Enjoyed baking soda experiment.

History

Enjoys historical literature! Attention span is growing listening to me read books to big brother. Answers most questions I ask brother. Likes to look at pictures. Always wants me to keep reading (unless he can go outside). Brings up info from stories at other times of day.

OBSERVATION NOTES

Social Studies
Interested in transportation, firemen, policemen. Discusses reason for holidays. Aware of environment. Recycles.

Fine Arts (Music, Art, Drama...)
Not interested in musical instrument. Enjoys singing with headphones on, but not with an audience. Likes to "create." Does not want to participate in school skits, talent night, etc. More interested in visual than in performing arts.

Health
Daily grooming habits are good. Brushes teeth, combs hair. (Need to work on "clean socks") Concerned with nutrition—interested in watching sweets & fats. (?????) Discusses importance of physical fitness for overall health.

Physical Fitness
Very active. Enjoys biking, roller blading, trampoline, swimming (a great deal at grandparents'). Likes sports day program. Better at movement than flexibility exercises.

OBSERVATION NOTES

Bible, Religious Training

Advancing well in Awana program. Follows pastor in church—asks questions about sermon. Participates well in family Bible reading. Verse memorization is quick, retention is good!

Additional Areas of Observation

_____

_____

_____

_____

_____

_____

_____

_____

_____

_____

_____

_____

_____

_____

_____

_____

_____

_____

_____

_____

_____

_____

_____

_____

Informal Handwriting Assessment

Ask the student to copy one or more of the following sentences in his best manuscript, italic or cursive or whichever form of penmanship he has been using in his writing. Each sentence has been designed to include all twenty-six letters of the English alphabet in lowercase. Be sure to have the student use the paper you would like him to be writing on when he has mastered the next level. For example, if he will continue writing on elementary-ruled paper for some time use that; however, if you expect him to begin writing on binder paper, use that for this pre-test.

1. A quick brown fox jumps over the lazy dogs.
2. Picking just six quinces, the new farmhand proves strong but lazy.
3. William said that everything about his jacket was in quite good condition except for the zipper.
4. The vixen jumped quickly on her foe, barking with zeal.

When your student has completed this assignment, use his handwriting sample to complete the "Handwriting Critique" shown on pages 95 and 174.

Place this sample in the student portfolio discussed on page 86. Plan in your teaching schedule to systematically repeat this procedure to evaluate progress and set new goals for penmanship.

Character Qualities Review

Student Name *Jason*   Evaluation Period *1st* qtr/1999

Character Quality	Weak	Improving	Satisfactory	Excellent
Attentiveness	✓			
Brotherly Love		✓		
Contentment			✓	
Courtesy			✓	
Cooperation		✓		
Dependability	✓			
Diligence	✓			
Following Directions	✓			
Forgiving				
Friendliness				
Gentleness				
Helpfulness				✓
Honesty		✓		
Humility		✓		
Industriousness	✓			
Integrity		✓		
Kindness			✓	
Neatness	✓			
Obedience			✓	
Perseverance		✓		
Prudence	✓			
Respectfulness				✓
Self-control		✓		

> You and your children might want to fill this out separately and then compare. It is helpful to know how our children perceive themselves in each of these character areas. Sometimes they know what they need to work on even before we tell them. Then you can affirm their strengths as well.

Student Inventory

Name _Kyle_   **Age** _10_   **Date** _12/29/98_

Subject or Skill	Excellent	Very Good	Pretty Good	Just O.K.	Not Very Good	Doesn't Apply
Bible		x				
Reading aloud		x				
Reading silently	x					
Vocabulary			x			
Writing organization	x					
Writing punctuation		x				
Creative writing		x				
Grammar and parts of speech					x	
Spelling		x				
Math - overall	x					
Addition	x					
Subtraction	x					
Multiplication	x					
Division	x					
Fractions, decimals, percentages		x				
Word problems		x				
History			x			
Government		x				
Geography		x				
Using maps, charts, and graphs			x			
Using reference materials to do research		x				
Science	x					
Health					x	
Physical fitness		x				
Art			x			
Music		x				
Drama	x					
Oral presentations	x					

PLAN

...to devise something to be done

"Where do we want to be?"

plan:
...to devise something to be done

"Where do we want to be?"

Now that you know where you and your students *are*, you can decide where you want to be by the end of the year/quarter/month or in two, three, or five years. It has often been said, "If you don't know where you are going, any road will take you there." It is important to decide *where* you want your students to be the next time you diagnose and evaluate them. Only then can you determine *how* you will go about reaching these goals.

This section is devoted to goal setting. This is where you decide what the *target* is. It is just as necessary to define clear, specific goals for the educator as for the student. Individualized Educational Programs (IEP) have been used in schools only for special education students, but you can provide your own special education for each child by setting individual goals in all areas. We include here some information and forms to help you do this. Another tool included here, the "Objectives & Evaluation Form," can also be used to plan and to evaluate. The marvelous benefit of projecting clearly defined goals is that you give yourself the opportunity to evaluate and diagnose continuously, not just when test time rolls around. On a daily basis you can determine whether you are on course or not. The scope and sequence discussed in the previous section should also be used to help you determine where to go next.

Props for Planning

Individualized Education Program (IEP)
Is exactly what it says. This is the specific plan you intend to implement in order to educate your children. It is designed to address their individual strengths and weaknesses.

Objectives
Specific, measurable goals set by you which enable you to track the progress you and your children are making.

Timelines
The larger assignment is broken down into bite-size tasks, and each is given a due date. This is useful for instructors and students alike. It helps you, the instructor, stay on track, and it helps your students learn to manage their time and plan their studies. The "Science Project Student Timeline" and the "Student Project Timeline" in the next section can also be used for goal setting.

Lists
Listing tasks to be done, skills to be addressed, concepts to be mastered, etc. is a great way to outline your objectives and keep moving toward them. A list, such as "Junior and Senior High Level Writing Assignments," lets you know which skills have been addressed and which still need instruction or practice. You needn't wait until your student is junior high age to begin using this checklist. Students are often completing some of these tasks by fourth or fifth grade or earlier.

Curriculum Scope and Sequence
A scope and sequence, such as the one included on pages 16 through 20 is an important tool. The scope and sequence details the course of study. The scope designates the content or concepts to be addressed. The sequence tells in which order they will be addressed. There are many sources of scope and sequence lists. They are available in various forms from textbook publishers, local school districts, curriculum suppliers, and even some private home-schooling organizations. You are certainly free to create your own; however, most parents feel it is helpful to have guidelines. If you choose to adopt a publisher's scope and sequence, remember it is only a guide. You are still free to make your own modifications and adapt it to your unique learning environment.

Activity Charts
Charting activities is a great way to plan, record, and review skills you want to address. The "Physical Education Record" on page 54 is an example of an activity chart. This can be done with any activity or group of activities on which you wish your students to spend time. It is especially helpful to teach your children to keep track of their own activity charts. This teaches them to take some responsibility for their own progress, and they can see what they have accomplished in the process.

Individualized Education Program (IEP)

Consider going to your physician for a check-up. What if you failed to pass the eye exam? Suppose your doctor said, "Well, every other thirty-seven year old can read this chart exactly this fast. You ought to be able to also. Please continue reading it until you get it right." The thought of that is absurd! Your doctor would, hopefully, send you to a specialist who could help correct your vision so that you could see as well as any other thirty-seven year old, or any seventeen year old for that matter. You need individualized help to maintain and enhance your vision.

At the same time, if your eye exam demonstrated 20/20 vision you would be shocked to have your doctor say, "Well, your eyes are fine, so the rest of you must be in perfect condition as well. That will be all, thanks." This is equally ridiculous. The fact that you have 20/20 vision does not mean your hearing, heart, reflexes, circulation, respiration, and digestive systems are all functioning properly. You expect your doctor to look at your bodily functions individually as well as wholly.

The same is true of your students. One size fits all education isn't very effective. Therefore, many parents and private teachers attempt to individualize student educational programs.

The Individualized Education Program, (IEP) in its purest form, is at the heart of home education and private tutoring. The IEP is often used to describe the individual student's course of study. The intent of the IEP is to create an "individualized" curriculum that addresses the specific needs and challenges of the student rather than relying upon a curriculum geared to the "average student."

Many states require formal IEPs for special education students. In a sense, every child should have an IEP whether or not the state requires it. Once a student's strengths and weaknesses have been diagnosed, it is relatively simple to plan what needs to be taught and which areas to remediate or enrich.

In traditional school settings, whether public or private, the IEP is regularly used for students considered to have special needs. For this reason it is often designed by a team of professionals. The team might include the classroom teacher, school psychologist, speech pathologist, the school principal, a special education supervisor, a medical professional, and the student's parent(s). This team begins by diagnosing the special needs and abilities of the student. Each member gives input based on his/her unique experience with the student and proposes programs, resources, and curriculum materials to be included in the student's overall educational program. The team synthesizes the information and develops an IEP.

The home-schooling parent or private tutor could follow the same process. Any individual involved in the student's life might have valuable input. You might interview the piano teacher, soccer coach, Bible club counselor, former school teacher/tutor, or grandparents. Remember their input is *only* an individual's opinion and is likely to be biased in one way or another. However, it can help you to see patterns and general strengths and weaknesses. This process might also confirm your direction. The benefit of this approach is that you, the parent, remain in control of what to do with the information you receive. You determine whether to discard it or incorporate it into your course of study. It will also help you know who is on your team as you move down the path of home education.

Now that you have done your research, you need to develop your student's IEP. Decide what subject and skill areas need to be addressed and on what level. In other words, your student might be third grade according to the age of his peers, while he has fifth-grade math skills and reads at a second-grade level. It does not make sense to plug him into a pre-packaged third-grade program. It will not challenge him in math and he will be frustrated in his reading. Likewise, he might struggle or excel with fine motor skills or physical agility or artistic endeavors. The purpose of the IEP is to first evaluate each skill area separately and then to design a program that addresses each area, yet one that works together as a cohesive unit.

Certainly it sounds easier to simply purchase the stack of books for the appropriate grade level. However, your student is an unique individual and he deserves to be educated as such. You will both be frustrated if he is not. The rewards of designing a program to custom fit your student are worth the effort.

The IEP forms on the following pages are designed to assist you in coordinating your student's IEP. They may appear redundant or seem private. Keep in mind that these are only suggestions for you to use in designing your own IEP. They resemble those used by many local and county, public and private schools. Remember, it is not your goal to stay in step with the local traditional school programs. However, it is always to your benefit to record and track your child's progress in a way that enables you to easily communicate his educational achievement when it becomes necessary and appropriate.

It is important to know what is required of you by your state. These regulations differ from state to state. While many states do require home-schooling parents to maintain an IEP, many do not. The following forms should enable you to satisfy most state regulations. If your state does not require that you design and maintain an IEP, don't overlook its benefits for you as your child's instructor. Remember, the more clearly you state the objectives, the easier it is to evaluate your student's progress . . . and your own!

EDUCATION

The bringing up as of a child; instruction; formation of manners. Education comprehends all that series of instruction and disciplines that is intended to enlighten the understanding, correct the temper, form the manners and habits of youth, and fit them for usefulness in their future stations. To give children a good education in manners, arts, and science is important; to give them a religious education is indispensable; and an immense responsibility rests on parents and guardians who neglect these duties.
Webster's American Dictionary of the English Language, 1828.

Individualized Education Program (IEP)
General Information

Student Name *Kenneth* Grade *3* Sex: M *x* F ____
School Year *1998 - 99* Birthdate *7/17/91*
Parent/Guardian Names *Scott & Suzy Smith*
Street Address *1234 Trancas St., Napa, CA 94558*
Mailing Address *same*
Telephone: Home *707-5432* Work *Dad 717-3421*
School Schedule: Traditional ____ Year Round *x*
Special Needs: The student has ____ has not *x* been diagnosed with special needs.
If you checked "has," complete the Special Education page of the IEP.
This IEP includes Student Success Study Team Evaluation Forms from the following individuals:

SAMPLE

Name	Relationship to student	Contact
Francis Frank	*Piano Teacher*	*Hm. Phone-987-6543*
Leon Canelli	*Soccer Coach*	*Napa Parks & Rec*
Charles Later	*Pastor*	*Hilltop Fellowship*
Bea Taponi	*Bible Club Leader*	*1st Christian Church*
Mary Brown	*Aunt/School Teacher*	*Hm Phone-234-5678*

The following diagnostic and assessment tools were used in developing objectives for this term and are attached:
WRAT (Wide Range Achievement Test), Diagnostic Writing Checklist, Bob Jones Post-Tests for Math & Grammar, Scope & Sequence

This IEP addresses the following areas of the student's development:

Reading x
Spelling x
Writing x
Reference x
Study Skills x
Organization Skills x

Math x
Science x
History x
Physical Fitness x
Life Skills x

Other
Spanish, Music, Physical Fitness, Art

IEP completed by *Suzy M. Smith* Relationship to student *Mother*
Mother's Signature *Suzy M. Smith* Father's Signature *Scott S. Smith*

Student Success Study Team
Individualized Education Program (IEP)

You have been asked to participate in this Student Success Study Team because you have participated in or observed some aspect of education and development for the following student: *Kenneth Smith*

Please complete the following information from your observations of this student to the best of your ability.

Teacher/Instructor Name: *Francis Frank*

Activities/Skills/Areas Observed: *Piano*

Present Levels of Performance

SAMPLE

Strengths

Kenneth catches on to new concepts & theory quickly, is eager to play, has a very good ear for music, and very good technique when he is focused. He does well in performance situations.

Concerns

Kenneth does well when he is focused. He can be distracted easily and then does not apply himself as well as he is capable of.

Significant Factors Contributing to Performance
(Social, Emotional, Health, Academic, Behavioral, Physical) Please be specific.

Strengths

Kenneth appears to be healthy & alert & I see no reason he should not continue to progress rapidly. He takes instruction well and receives constructive comments and uses them.

Concerns

Kenneth does overreact at times and is a bit of a perfectionist.

From my observations and interactions, I believe the following actions would help this student continue to progress: *Continue lessons and increase daily practice time to frequent short practices instead of long sesions, Continue working on theory and music history.*

Signature *Francis Frank*   Date   *8/2/99*

Individualized Education Program (IEP)
Annual Goals & Methods

Name __Stuart_____ Grade __3__

Goal Setting Date ___8/15/98___ Anticipated Completion Date ___6/2/99___

These goals may be taken from a scope and sequence like the one included on pages 16-20 or from the curriculum resources you have chosen for this school year.

They should also be based on the results of the diagnosing you have done so far.

SAMPLE

Subject	Objective	Obj. Met	Method	Materials	Level
Bible	Read & understand Bible truths	6/15	Individual & corporate reading	Bible for Children	NA
Literature	*Read 2,000 pages from curriculum list *Identify character, setting & plot *Recognize major characteristics of literature - poetry, fables, fairy tales, plays, fiction, etc.	4/25 2/23 3/12	Independent reading & discussion	Attached Reading List	3
Comprehension	*Draw conclusions/main ideas/supporting details from material read *Recall facts from reading	9/23 9/24	Reading Comp. wb & Reading together	McGuffey's 2nd & 3rd What Every 3rd Grader Needs...Hirsch	3
Grammar	*complete Bob Jones third grade Scope & Sequence	6/7	Teacher instruction & Workbook	Bob Jones Grammar 3	3
Arithmetic	*Complete grade three curriculum *Master +, -, x facts to 12	5/15 4/13	Workbook/ Instruction/ Flash cards/ Manipulatives	Bob Jones Math 3 Frank Schaeffer Math Arithmetic Minute Drills	3
History	*Retell, relate highlights from Early American History *Explain their relevance to life today *Recognize God's direction of people and events	11/27 1/15 11/27	*Literature *Responding to lit. in writing	*Beautiful Feet Books, Early American History Study Guide	3
Geography	*Be able to read maps *Create maps incl. legends *Chart routes on map *Recognize geographical features in NE US	2/14 3/12 3/12 3/31	*Literature *Map making *Teacher instruction	Paddle to the Sea	3

Individualized Education Program (IEP)
Annual Goals & Methods, page 2

Subject	Objective	Obj. Met	Method	Materials	Level
Study Reference Skills	*Use Table of Contents, Index, Glossary *Use dictionary skills, alphabetizing, definitions *Use phone book & newspaper	2/16 10/21 12/6	Teacher directed activities	*Literature *Dictionary *Phone book *Newspaper *Unit Study supplements	3
Composition	*Write stories, reports, essays, poems, speeches *know characteristics of good oral presentation	5/14 11/15	*Daily journal writing *Weekly compositions *Public Speaking Class	*Teacher-planned assignments *Public Speaking class notebook	3
Life Skills	*Carry out household chores, laundry, trash, pet care, sweeping, gardening	6/6	*Daily checklists *Parent instruction	Household items	NA
Music	*Learn to play simple tunes on violin *Gain appreciation for classical composers	12/23 3/24	*Violin practice *Reading, keeping notebook of composers	*Violin Lessons *Color the Classics	NA
Spanish	*Say & read greetings, colors, animals, foods, counting, family names	4/14	Teacher instruction	Teacher-planned lessons	NA
Science	*Understand electricity, electronics	5/25	indiv reading & reports	The Way Things Work, Macauley	NA
Cooking	*Basic cooking skills, safety & nutrition	2/27	4-H class	Teacher planned	NA
Sewing	*Basic sewing skills	11/17	4-H class	Teacher planned	NA
Physical Fitness	*Swimming *Improve physical fitness skills *Team sports	9/23 6/7 6/7	*Swim class *President's Physical Fitness Program	*President's Physical Fitness Booklet & Record	NA

Individualized Education Program (IEP)
Special Education

SAMPLE

Student Name ___Jon Poplin___

Describe the disability:

___ADHD - - Attention Deficit w/ Hyperactivity Disorder___

The disability was diagnosed by (doctor/counsellor) ___Dr. Nelson___

Date of diagnosis ___7/16/99___

Method of diagnosis (tests used, etc.) ___Refer to medical cum from Dr office___

What is the difference between his/her level of achievement and the level expected at his/her age? ___approximately 1.5 grade levels___

What sources, public or private, are currently being used to address this child's needs? ___private tutoring___

Check all handicapping conditions which apply below:

☐ Mentally Retarded   ☐ Other Health Impaired
☐ Hard of Hearing   ☐ Deaf Blind
☐ Deaf   ☐ Multi-Handicapped
☐ Speech/Language Impaired   ☐ Autistic
☐ Visually Impaired   ☐ Traumatic Brain Injury
☐ Seriously Emotionally   ☐ Specific Learning Disability: Disturbed
☐ Orthopedically Impaired   ___ADHD___

Student needs the following equipment: ___none___

Student is using the following medication: ___none___

Student has been using this/these medications since (date): ___none___

Completed by ___Sharon Dodd___   Relationship to student ___mother___

EDUCATOR'S OBJECTIVES *SAMPLE*

OBJECTIVE	METHOD Be as specific as you can. List book titles, people's names, conventions, etc.	INTENDED COMPLETION
gain confidence in decision to home school	Read *The Right Choice--Home Schooling*, Klicka	9/30
look ahead to jr. high	Read *The High School Handbook*, Schofield	1/5
get help with teaching reading & writing	Attend a teaching reading seminar in the area	10/15
get organized	Read *Mrs. Mom: Agonized or Organized* Debe Haller, B. Bennett	11/15
nutritious meals	Locate & purchase a healthy cookbook & schedule 2 days a month for menu planning/ cooking	10/1
get to know curriculum options for next year	Attend home school convention/curriculum fair	7/9
better handle on planning curriculum	Purchase Cathy Duffy's *Christian Home Educator's Curriculum Manual*	2/1
incorporate more hands-on science	Talk with Jane about a monthly science coop	9/30

OBJECTIVES & EVALUATION FORM

Student Name *Justin*   Evaluation Period *3rd*

Specific Objectives	Mastered	Satisfactory Progress	Needs More Work	Not Addressed
Character Development *follow directions 1st time* *consistent with please & thank-you*	x x			
treat brother with consideration			x	
demonstrate patience when I'm working with brother		x		
follow Mom's directions as quickly as Dad's	x			
Bible & Christian Training				
memorize at least 1 verse/week	x			
follow in family Bible reading w/ o distractions or interruptions	x			
be able to locate books of the Bible		x		
Language Arts (reading, phonics, grammar, composition, spelling, vocabulary, penmanship)				
penmanship—even letters *sit still*		x		
spell independently		x		
write legibly enough to read it back		x		
extend attention span in silent reading	x			
improve use of decoding	x			
improve use of context clues for meaning	x			

OBJECTIVES & EVALUATION FORM
Page 2

Specific Objectives	Mastered	Satisfactory Progress	Needs More Work	Not Addressed
Arithmetic				
Improve + and - facts to 95% accuracy in 5 min on drills	x			
Be able to tell time on face clock		x		
Art				
Continue creating with new medium				x
Incorporate across the curriculum			x	
Music				
Work on singing			x	
Use "Meet the Master" to develop appreciation		x		
PE/Health				
Daily P.E. time Nutrition study combined w/meal plan		x x		
Life Skills				
Study earthquake safety & preparedness		x		
Know fire safety rules		x		
Social Studies (history, geography, etc.)				
Be able to explain 4 diff. world views		x		
Memorize & locate continents, oceans			x	
Science				
Complete a science project for science fair	x			

Junior & Senior High Level
Writing Assignments

Note: These writing activities may come from any area of the curriculum, or family life. It is not necessary to complete them in order. They may be incorporated into the curriculum over a period of two or three years depending upon when you begin.

Writing Project	Due Date	Date Completed
List	1-5	1-5
Memo	1-19	1-18
Journal	10/15-1/19	1-23
Short Story	1-26	1-26
Summary	2-2	2-5
Observations	2-2	2-5
Dialogue	2-9	2-9
Sketch	2-9	2-10
Report	2-9	2-12
Book Review	2-16	2-16
Movie Review	2-16	2-17
News Article	2-23	3-4
Friendly Letter	10-1	10-7
Business Letter	1-5	1-5
Letter to the Editor	11-3	11-3
Poetry	*small group study*	
Essay: Autobiographical Incident	4-6	4-6
Essay: First-Hand Biography	4-18	4-18
Essay: Memoir	5-2	5-2
Essay: Evaluation	5-11	5-10
Essay: Problem-Solution	5-21	5-21
Essay: Analysis/Speculation	6-2	6-4

Physical Education Record

Name *Chelsea*   Evaluation Period *9/97-7/99*

Activity	✓ = 20 minutes								A = Attempted Exercise				
walking	✓	✓	✓	✓	✓	✓	✓	✓	✓	✓	✓		
jogging	✓	✓	✓	✓	✓	✓	✓	✓					
stretching	✓	✓	✓	✓	✓	✓	✓	✓					
sit-ups	36	42	41	45	53	55	62	65	6?	6?	6?	7?	7?
pull-ups	A	A	A	A	A	1	1	1	2	2	2	2	3
push-ups	15	15	13	15	17	17	19	17	19	11	21	20	19
throw & catch softball	✓	✓	✓	✓	✓	✓	✓	✓	✓	✓			
jump rope	✓	✓	✓	✓	✓	✓	✓	✓	✓	✓			
bicycling	✓	✓	✓	✓	✓	✓	✓	✓	✓	✓	✓	✓	✓
roller blading/ skating	✓	✓	✓	✓	✓	✓	✓	✓	✓	✓	✓	✓	✓
shooting baskets	✓	✓	✓	✓	✓	✓	✓	✓	✓	✓			
swimming	✓	✓	✓	✓	✓	✓	✓	✓	✓	✓			
kicking (kick ball or soccer)	✓	✓	✓	✓	✓	✓	✓	✓	✓	✓	✓	✓	✓
snow sports	✓	✓	✓	✓	✓	✓	✓	✓					
trampoline	✓	✓	✓	✓	✓	✓	✓	✓	✓	✓	✓	✓	✓
tumbling	✓	✓	✓	✓	✓	✓	✓	✓	✓	✓	✓	✓	✓

This table is used to keep track of the variety of physical activities in which you want your student to participate. You choose your own activities. Recording them in writing and tracking student participation helps you to stay on track. It is a way of planning what you want your student to accomplish as well as charting your progress toward meeting your objectives. The table provided in the Appendix allows you to determine your own goals for physical activity. Some included in this list may not be important to you, while others, not listed here, are a part of your family's regular routine. You may track student activity for any period of time. This student was charted over two school years.

GUIDE

...lead, instruct, direct, regulate, manage

"What will we do?"

guide:
...*lead,*
instruct, direct,
regulate, manage

"What will we do?"

Now that you have diagnosed *where* you *are* and decided where you want to *be*, you must develop a plan for *how* to get there. This is where your methods and materials come in. Too often educators let the books and resources used to carry out a course of study determine what the goals ought to be. No thought is given to where children begin or where they should end up.

You have taken the time to diagnose a starting point and plan some important goals. Now you can make informed decisions about how to reach them. Don't be afraid to alter your course at this point. Perhaps you discovered you have jumped over skills or important content that needs to be filled in. Maybe you are spending precious time reviewing material that has already been mastered. Whatever the case, remember the curriculum is your tool and do not be enslaved to it.

Sometimes God has a better plan, and He presents a wonderful learning opportunity that we had not planned into our schedule. Seize these opportunities; they're likely to be the highlights of your home schooling. Don't let your carefully planned goals interfere with meaningful opportunities. In fact, you should build some flex time into your schedule, expecting such opportunities to arise.

GUIDELINES THAT GAUGE . . .

Many diagnostic tools can also be used to gauge or measure student progress in addition to diagnosing current skills and abilities. For example, by taking notes as you observe your student, you can compare these with future observations to see whether progress has been made. In discussing the content or subject matter with your student, you might find he understands much more (or no better) than in a previous discussion. By re-giving the pre-test as a post-test you can compare results and see specific concepts, skills, etc. that have been improved upon. This also serves as a guide to help us determine which areas need more or less attention.

Guidelines are extremely helpful in gauging student progress. If students do not clearly understand what skills they are supposed to demonstrate, they will not know why you say they are or are not showing improvement. (Neither will you.) This can be a very frustrating experience.

Note that you can also use some of the tools in this section to help you separate effort or attitude from the actual merits of the work accomplished. This can be done in any area of the curriculum. You can also adapt the effort portion of a grade to reflect whether the work is done individually or carried out in cooperation with a small group. Use tools for evaluating effort to establish clear expectations which will serve to guide both you and your students.

There are a number of ways to establish guidelines by which to direct and measure student progress. Following are just a few of the many ways to guide students and teachers in planning to progress.

Clear Detailed Expectations
The "Oral Presentation," "Essay," and "Writing Guidelines" are included as examples of writing out clear expectations for the student so that both student and teacher have in mind the same goals.

Timeline of Tasks
The "Science Project Student Timeline" is included as a sample of presenting the student with clear directions so evaluation, including grading, becomes simple. This can be applied to any area of the curriculum, for special projects, student/teacher contracts, or for students who want truly *independent* study. This same form could be used (possibly requiring a number of pages) to outline details for an entire course. We've included master forms for both the "Science Project" and a more generic "Student Project Timeline."

Course Outline

These are clear-cut guidelines with points assigned for completing each project or assignment within the context of a larger project. This is similar to a rubric, but in addition, specific points are assigned that can be translated into a grade or percentage of work completed. Examples for public speaking and music course outlines are included. These might be used to outline just about any course you might teach.

Both the "Book Projects" and the "Literature Project" included here are examples of this type of system applied on a smaller scale. *The High School Handbook*, by Mary Schofield lays out a number of examples to help you design your own course of study.

Guidelines for Choices

Guidelines sometimes function as choices or suggestions for our children. For example, with young children, you might select books to which you would like to introduce them and put them all on one shelf. Children could be instructed to select a book from that shelf each day. We might assign older students to choose one "Book Project Idea" per month or to select books from at least six different genres this semester (refer to the "Reading Genres" list in this section). Students might be given an "Approved Book List" and assigned a number of pages or books per quarter, semester, or year to be read and used in various projects.

You might enjoy using some of these examples to help you write your own delight directed studies in many areas of the curriculum.

Scope and Sequence as a Guide

The scope and sequence previously discussed can also be used as an ongoing guideline. The "Math Skills Checklist" shows how we can adapt any scope and sequence to keep track of when we introduce a new topic, practice and review the topic, and when a student actually masters the topic.

ORAL PRESENTATION STUDENT GUIDELINES

Prepare a short story or poem. Your reading or recitation must meet the following requirements:

♦ One to two minutes in length
♦ The subject of the poem or story must be clear.
♦ It must be a published work.
♦ You may read or recite but be sure you are familiar enough with the content to use as much expression as possible.

It is to be presented at the following date and time: May 5, 1999

Your presentation will be evaluated for:

Requirement	Points Possible	Points Earned
Being prepared on time	10	10
Beginning and ending with confidence	10	7
Poise	10	8
Eye contact	10	8
Articulation	10	8
Expression	10	8
Projection (volume)	10	7
Appropriate theme	20	10
Staying within the time allotted	10	10
Total	100	76

Your grade will be based on points earned. You are not being compared to anyone else. You are being compared to the best that you are capable of in each area. *Your preparation* will determine the quality of your presentation.

Grading Scale:

95 points = A
90 points = A-
85 points = B
80 points = B-

75 points = C+
70 points = C
Below this point you obviously did not prepare and will be required to present this material at the following date and time_____

See companion evaluation forms in the next section: "Poetry Reading/Recitation" and "Public Speaking Evaluation."

Notes for using the

Format For a One Page Essay

Parent/Teacher Notes:

♦ Use this format both to *guide* and *evaluate* student writing.

♦ To expand the assignment from a five-paragraph essay to include more information, direct your student to expand section II, the Body of the Paper. In place of three sentences, he should include three paragraphs about each point.

♦ The same format can be used to help your student write an outline before writing the essay. The same point system can also be used for the outline.

♦ You might write the points on the actual student essay where they apply.

♦ Use a grading schedule similar to the "Public Speaking Syllabus" or the "Book Projects" to convert points into a grade.

♦ If the essay is being evaluated for more than one component, (e.g., content, mechanics, and style), you can use a different color pen to assign points to each component as you write on the essay.

♦ This format and the suggested points are intended for use when emphasizing content. Once the student demonstrates that he understands how to organize the content of an essay, move to mechanics or style. Future essays should always be evaluated for proper organization of content.

♦ When evaluating for more than content, consider the following point allotment:

   40 points content
   30 points mechanics
   30 points style
 100 points = Total   *Grade is based on percentage of 100 points.*

♦ Once the format is understood, refer to the "Writing Critique," page 99, or the "Writing Mechanics and Punctuation" form, page 97, to assist with evaluating writing.

Student Notes:

♦ Your points should be three things about the topic which are related but different.

♦ You need to say three things about each point which are related but different.

♦ A clearly stated topic sentence will make the entire paper easier to follow.

♦ Vary sentence beginnings to make your paper more interesting.

♦ To expand your essay to include more information expand section II, the Body of the Paper. In place of three sentences, include three paragraphs about each point.

Format for One Page Essay
Emphasis on *Content*

Title
(Appropriate for the essay topic) (10 points)

I. Introductory Paragraph
   A. Topic Sentence (State what the paper is about.) (15)
   B. Three things you intend to say about the topic
      1. (5)
      2. (5)
      3. (5)
II. Body of the Paper
   A. Paragraph 2
      Three things about point #1
      1. (5)
      2. (5)
      3. (5)

   B. Paragraph 3
      Three things about point #2
      1. (5)
      2. (5)
      3. (5)
   C. Paragraph 4
      Three things about point #3
      1. (5)
      2. (5)
      3. (5)
III. Summary of the Paper (15)
   A. Draw a conclusion, e.g., "Something I learned in this study . . ."
      (restate in your own words), *and/or*
   B. Summarize your points, *and/or*
   C. Restate the topic sentence in different words

Writing Guidelines

Consider this scene. Your fifth grader has been asked to complete a report on "The Life of George Washington." It was assigned weeks ago. After several interruptions in the family's school schedule, you discovered it was due yesterday. Your student has complained that he was not given enough notice to complete the assignment. You counter that he has had several weeks. He maintains that there have been a number of interruptions and that you are not being fair. After cutting off the argument and setting a final deadline, you now have a writing project in your hands. In addition to being late and sloppy, your son's attitude about school work in general is less than tolerable. Surely, he cannot deserve more than a 'D' on this assignment.

Upon receiving his grade, your son questions your methods. After all, he poses, you didn't tell him you wanted more information about Washington's childhood education. He doesn't know how to draw pictures very well, so the stick figures ought to do, and he has never drawn a map before. Since this is his first "real" report, he reminds you, he thought you would be more understanding. Before you know it, you are negotiating his grade. After an exhausting duel, you collapse onto the family room sofa, wondering whether you are competent to continue teaching him yourself.

Your daughter, on the other hand, has difficulty spelling, doesn't retain information she has read independently, and struggles to follow written directions. However, her report is neat, has a very pretty cover, and besides, she offered to help with the baby so you could have a few quiet moments at your desk. Surely, she deserves an A-.

You have just taught your son to argue for his reward. You have trained your daughter that it doesn't matter what she accomplishes as long as it looks cute and she acts sweet. Furthermore, you have needlessly reinforced your own lack of confidence in your ability to teach and train your own children. All of this could be avoided with a little advance planning and a few well-laid out guidelines.

It is important to consider the purpose of a writing assignment when the assignment is given. When you know the purpose of the activity, it is much easier to evaluate the student's performance. If you are looking for attitude and effort, say so. If you are looking for writing skills, they need to be clearly specified. If it's specific content you are after, spell it out, so both you and your student know what is expected.

The tools offered for such subjective areas of study as writing, speaking, research reports, and literature studies, to name a few, are intended to take the guesswork out of grading and evaluating student performance. In addition, you, the teacher, have a clear idea how to guide your student through a project, including budgeting his time and organizing his work.

Guidelines to Critique Writing

The following guidelines correlate to the "Writing Critique" included in the next section. The "Writing Critique" will be helpful for many beginning writing projects. When you are looking for a more thorough demonstration of mechanics and punctuation, it is suggested that you use the "Writing Mechanics and Punctuation Evaluation." If you are emphasizing writing format, you may prefer to use the "Essay Format Guidelines."

Promptness: The assignment is given a specific deadline, including date and time. For example, Thursday morning, Oct. 31 at 9:30 a.m. This means that at 9:31 a.m. the assignment is late and at least 1 point is deducted. Decide how many points per minute, hour or day will be deducted. After the first time a student loses all his points for promptness and it affects his letter grade, he will make an effort to finish on time. In our home, it takes a family conference to move a deadline once it has been set. This teaches our children to plan around piano recitals, birthday parties and speech tournaments.

Neatness: The paper has a neat and orderly presentation. The student has used his best penmanship. It might be helpful to compare this paper to a portfolio sample of the student's best writing so far. The title or cover, if applicable, is neat and attractive. The student plans his space so that words fit on the same line, etc.

Content: List the specific information you are looking for. The more detailed your directions, the easier it is for the student and you to determine whether they were followed. For example, state that you would like to know three things about George Washington's childhood education and three positions he held in the service of our country with descriptions of each.

Expression: This refers to the way ideas are expressed. Does the student use interesting vocabulary? Does he start each sentence with a different word? Does he use adjectives and adverbs to describe what you are talking about? Does he state his points clearly in a way that is easy for the reader to follow? Does he use effective transitions instead of jumping from one idea to the next?

Mechanics: See the "Mechanics and Punctuation Evaluation." All or a portion might be evaluated in a given assignment.

Graphics: This means any illustrations, charts, maps, graphs, cover pages, or fancy titles. Are they neat? Organized? Colorful? Appropriate? Interesting? Accurate? Detailed?

Extra Credit: Does the student go beyond the minimum requirements? Award extra credit if he provides 2 maps instead of 1; writes 3 pages instead of 2; reports on 6 varieties instead of 4; adds a graph or chart that was not assigned; and, perhaps, turns the project in early (by a specified date). All extra credit must be approved in advance.

Sample Writing Assignment

Assignment: Write an eleven-paragraph paper discussing the formation of our country's constitution. Follow the format described on the "Essay Format" page. Attach finished assignment to a "Writing Critique."

Your paper will be evaluated for:
Promptness: (10) Due Mon., Nov. 11, 9:30 a.m.

Neatness: (10) Use your best cursive handwriting. Pages should be neat and clean with very few erasures, (not more than three per page).

Content: (20) Compare and contrast the original Thanksgiving with our current-day celebration. Be sure to address:
✓ foods: types and how they are prepared
✓ festivities: how the holiday is/was celebrated
✓ people: those that celebrate together and their reasons for doing so
✓ setting: location and accommodations
✓ spirit of the holiday: the meaning of this occassion.

Expression: (20) Vary sentence beginnings. Add adjectives and adverbs to make your paper more interesting.

Mechanics: (20) Special attention will be paid to capitals, commas, ending punctuation, and spelling.

Graphics: (20) Create an attractive cover with the title of your paper. Decorate it in a theme that is appropriate for your content. Also include a chart or graph comparing some aspect of the two types of celebrations.

SCIENCE PROJECT
STUDENT TIMELINE

Activity	Due Date	Date Completed
Choose a topic that you are interested in.*** Write out your topic.	1-5	1-5
Collect books, information, and reference materials to research your topic. List your research materials.		1-18
Write a report summarizing your research.	1-19	1-23
Make a list of everything you will need to do in order. Include all the supplies you will need to carry out your project.	1-26	1-26
Write out the procedure for your experiment or demonstration.	2-2	2-5
Write a hypothesis. What do you predict will happen?	2-2	2-5
Gather your materials. Get everything ready to carry out your experiment or demonstration.	2-9	2-9
Perform your experiment or practice your demonstration.	2-9	2-10
Record your observations	2-9	2-12
What did you learn or find out by doing this experiment? Record your conclusions in writing.	2-16	2-16
Compare your conclusions to your original hypothesis.	2-16	2-17
Prepare your display. Present the information you collected in easy-to-read graphs or tables.	2-23	3-4
Prepare a two- to three-minute oral presentation.	3-1	3-7
*** First Discuss project proposal with Mom and Dad	1-5	1-5

SAMPLE

STUDENT PROJECT TIMELINE

May be used to guide students through projects in nearly any area of study.

Activity	Due Date	Date Complete/ Points
Choose a topic related to early American history that you are interested in. Be sure the topic area is broad enough to complete the tasks assigned in this project timeline. Write a brief description of your topic area. (5 points)	1-5	1-5 5
Collect books, information, and reference materials to research your topic area. List all research materials that you use during this project. (5)	1-*SAMPLE*	
Outline the main points you intend to address within your topic area. (10)	1-19	1-23 9
Create a chart or graph that gives information about your topic area. (10)	1-26	1-26 9
Illustrate part of your topic area in a drawing, painting, sculpture, or another art form of your choice. (10)	2-2	2-5 9
Imagine you are someone from the time period, physical setting, industry, etc. of your topic area. Write a letter to another person giving details of daily life or describing an important historical event. (10)	2-2	2-5 9
Complete the written portion of your project. Each point in your outline should become a separate page in the report. Use the "One Page Essay Format" to help you with this. (20)	2-9	2-9 17
Invent something that could have been useful to the people, place, industry, etc. you are addressing in your report. Either create it or draw a detailed picture of it. Include a written explanation of the changes this invention would have brought about. (15)	2-9	2-10 14
Create a crossword puzzle using vocabulary from your research and words that are unique to your topic area. (5)	2-16	2-17 4
Prepare a three to five-minute oral presentation. Incorporate your charts, graphs, and illustrations. (10)	3-1	3-7 9

GRADE _____ 90

Public Speaking Course Outline

Area of Evaluation	**Points**

Effort

Assignments completed promptly	10
Discussion	15
Respect for parent/instructor	15
Ability to give and receive constructive comments	15
Courtesy toward other students	15
Preparation for presentations or discussion	15
Following directions	15

Achievement

Reading/Recitation	100
Impromptu	200
(4 opportunities worth 50 points each)	
Humor	100
Expository Speaking with Visual Aids	100
Persuasive Speaking	100
Public Speaking Quiz	100
Dramatic/Humorous Interpretation	100
Final Presentations	200

Both Effort and Achievement grades will be assigned at the end of the course.

<table>
<tr><td><u>Effort Scale</u></td><td><u>Achievement Scale</u></td></tr>
<tr><td>95 + points = A</td><td>930 + points = A</td></tr>
<tr><td>90 + points = A-</td><td>900 + points = A-</td></tr>
<tr><td>85 + points = B</td><td>830 + points = B</td></tr>
<tr><td>80 + points = B-</td><td>800 + points = B-</td></tr>
<tr><td>75 + points = C</td><td>750 + points = C</td></tr>
<tr><td>70 + points = C-</td><td>700 + points = C-</td></tr>
<tr><td>Below 70 points receives a failing grade and student is expected to repeat all or a portion of the course.</td><td>Below 700 points receives failing grade.</td></tr>
</table>

SAMPLE

Course Outline
Music

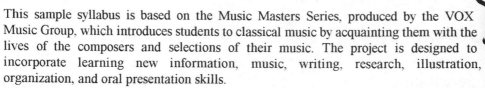

This sample syllabus is based on the Music Masters Series, produced by the VOX Music Group, which introduces students to classical music by acquainting them with the lives of the composers and selections of their music. The project is designed to incorporate learning new information, music, writing, research, illustration, organization, and oral presentation skills.

Activity	Points Received
Listen to each tape. (21 tapes) (2 pts. each = 42)	42
Set up a notebook of composers. (10)	10
Include the following information for each composer:	xxxxx
Summary of the composer's life (5 pts. each =105)	100
Describe the style of music he composed (2 pts. each = 42)	31
Title s of two pieces you especially enjoyed with a brief description of what attracts you to these particular pieces. (10 pts. each = 20)	18
Include a glossary of terms. Add one new word from each composer. (1 pt. each = 21)	20
Choose two composers and write an essay to compare and contrast them. Be sure to address their personal lives, their religious beliefs, and their music. (20)	15
Choose one composer you especially enjoyed. Write a 2-page research report about him. Include a chart or illustration of your choice. (20)	16
Give an oral presentation approximately ten minutes in length. Share as much information from your project as you can. Plan to share one or two musical selections as well. (20)	18
Total Points (300 possible) Percentage Score	270 90%

Reading Comprehension

Is it necessary to give a written examination in order to know our children comprehend what they have read? How much do our children need to write about what they read? How do we know they are retaining what they are reading? Is it necessary for us to read each and every page of each and every book, each and every one of our children is assigned? If we don't, how is it possible to evaluate their understanding?

These are just a few of the questions we as parents have about how to use the many reading materials to which we want to expose our children in the course of their education. In order to answer them, we need to consider *our* purposes for having *our* children read to begin with.

Reasons for Reading

Enjoyment: One of the by-products of teaching our children to read should be that they learn to enjoy reading. We encourage this by creating an environment that fosters reading. Family reading encourages interaction and exposes children to literature they cannot yet tackle alone. Helping our students choose materials they will find interesting helps as well. When enjoyment is the purpose, the last thing we want to do is require a lengthy, tedious, written report that might negate all the positive benefits achieved so far. A number of the "Book Project Ideas" are designed with enjoyment in mind. Remember, sometimes it is enough to simply enjoy the book!

Reading Skills: Our children need some specific skills in order to really enjoy their personal reading experiences. Until they can read fluently, both aloud and silently, they are limited, and their efforts can feel more laborious than fun. If your purpose in reading is to develop skills such as decoding, using context clues, reading for meaning, etc. don't expect your child to create elaborate projects and reports out of the reading. Each reading experience will very likely supply its own evaluation. As you listen to your child read, then discuss with him what he has read; you can tell whether he is sounding out words better this week than he did last week and whether he is grasping the main idea and meaning of words.

Information: Our children must also learn to read for information. They should research many different topics, using a variety of reference materials as they study. You can often evaluate this skill by asking questions and using the discussion and interview techniques described in the diagnostic section. At some point they need to learn to record information they have uncovered. This might require an essay, written report, research project, or oral presentation. Many tools included in these pages can help with each of these tasks.

Experience: There are many situations in life which we will never experience, some good, some bad. We can read about a great deal that we cannot experience first hand. Sometimes the experience of reading is enough. Other times you will want to check for understanding. You might choose book projects which will help you with this. Also consider *what* you are wanting your student to experience. If it is a culture or a time period, choose a project that helps him focus on that. If it is someone's situation in life, choose projects that emphasize those issues.

Writing Development: Good writers are almost always good readers—those who have read many different authors and have been influenced by their skill in word handling. One of the purposes of selecting good literature for our children to read is to expose them to the best writing so that they, too, can learn to construct beautiful and effective sentences. If that is the purpose for reading the selected literature, you will want to choose evaluation projects in which the student will demonstrate an understanding of the elements of writing. Essays, discussions, and oral presentations are good ways to evaluate an understanding of the elements of writing.

Vocabulary Enrichment: Of course we want our children to acquire and use appropriate vocabulary to communicate their ideas clearly. One of the best ways to build vocabulary is to choose literature that challenges them to comprehend more difficult words. These words then begin to show up in student speech and writing. I once advised parents who were concerned about their children's low vocabulary scores on a standardized achievement test. I counseled them not to purchase a vocabulary workbook, but instead to raise the level of literature their children were expected to read. As a result, in ten months' time, their test scores were raised two grade levels. If it is vocabulary you want to enrich, you should urge the student to interact with richer vocabulary in good literature.

Discerning Truth: Faith, values, morals, and beliefs are evident in most written material. Everything we expect or allow our children to read either confirms or opposes the truths we want them to hold onto. It is important that our children learn to discern whether or not an author is writing from the same worldview their family holds. If this is either a primary or secondary purpose for making a reading selection, be sure you evalute the reading for this element. Discussion is an important component in developing the ability to discern truth.

As our children become more proficient readers we begin to take a multipurpose approach to reading. We might choose reading material because it reinforces what they're studying in history or science. At the same time we can use it to expand their vocabulary and broaden their experience.

The projects we choose for evaluation should reflect as many of our purposes as possible but ought to emphasize what we are specifically targeting. Certainly there are many ways to assess our childrens' abilities to read and comprehend. A number of them are listed in the "Book Project Ideas" on the following pages.

Book Project Ideas

Formerly known as dull and boring book reports, these might be considered for any area of the curriculum in which students are reading.

Narration: Retell the story aloud. Be sure to include main characters and events. Point out your favorite part.

Interview: Pretend you are a reporter for a local news station. (Decide whether it is TV or radio.) Interview a character from the book. You may choose a main character or one that is on the sidelines. Develop a list of questions and decide what his/her responses would be based upon what you read.

Act Out Your Interview: Find someone to be the interviewer or the character and act out your interview. Better still . . . video or audio tape it for a later presentation.

Crossword Puzzle: Choose several (say 20 - 30) vocabulary words which were a stretch for you. Create a crossword puzzle using simple definitions for the clues. (Give your crossword to a friend and see if he can complete it.)

Illustrate: Draw, color, paint, sketch, or chalk your favorite scene from the story. Be sure to include as much detail as possible.

Mobile I: Use a coat hanger to create a mobile of all the characters in the story. Put the main characters on the hanger and attach supporting characters with yarn. Draw or color the character's profile on one side and tell about him/her on the reverse side.

Mobile II: Same as before, except include setting, plot, characters, theme, style, etc.

Research: Do some research to learn more about the author, setting, culture, time period, real people, and events, or the illustrator. Write a summary of your findings.

Skit: Find a few people to help you act out one or more scenes from the story. (You might even be able to do it alone – "a one-man show!") Once again, video it if you can.

Finish It: About halfway through the book, quit reading and write your own ending for the story. Be sure to resolve the conflict in the plot.

Add-A-Character: Invent a character who wasn't included in the story but who you think would belong. Write about how things might have happened differently had your character been on the scene.

Become-A-Character: Add yourself to the story. If you were the main character or one of the supporting characters, how would you handle one or more situations differently? Describe it in your writing.

Sing About It: Write a song that includes the highlights of the book and the main characters. Sing it. Record it. Get a few friends to sing it and record it with you. What kind of instruments would the characters have used? Can you find some of these instruments to use?

Compose Theme Music: If you play a musical instrument, this is for you. Movies have theme music. Create your own musical composition to reflect the theme of the story. Is it playful? suspenseful? mysterious? fantasy? Perform your musical arrangement for an audience of friends and family. Explain your inspiration for the composition.

Solution: Do you have a better solution to the conflict(s) presented in the plot? Write it out. How many people and events would have been affected if your solution had taken place? How would their lives have been different?

Rent the Movie: Has this book been made into a movie? If so, rent the video and watch it. Then compare and contrast the book to the video in writing or in discussion.

News Article: Write an article for a local newspaper about a major event in the story. Be sure to interview any key witnesses!

Magazine Article: How would your article be different if you were writing for a magazine instead of a newspaper? Which magazine are you writing it for?

Tabloid News: Would your news article be different if you were writing it for the tabloids? Try it.

Become the Main Character: . . . or any character for that matter. Dress up like one of the characters from the book and tell about your life. Describe some of your experiences. You can wait for a real, live audience or video tape your presentation.

Build It: Select a building from the setting to construct. Build it out of pretzels, gum drops, marshmallows, jelly beans, raisins, lincoln logs, toothpicks, clay, sticks, grass, weeds, or whatever works!

Review It: Write a book review. Read a couple of book reviews from a magazine to which your family subscribes and then write your own.

Consider submitting it to the magazine.

Become a Critic: If it's good enough for Ebert. . . . Present a review of the book the way the critics review movies and shows. Be sure to point out how the author's style did or didn't get the message across.

Promote It: Design a poster that would entice people to read it, much like a movie poster. Include pictures and words that are sure to hook others into reading the book.

Collage: Create a collage by cutting pictures out of magazines. Choose a theme—one of the main characters, the setting, or highlights of the book.

Game Show: Create "game show" questions and answers based on the book. Ask detailed questions about the characters, plot, setting, author, etc. Invite friends and family who have read the book to play your game show.

Whodunit?: Retell a portion of the plot as a mystery. Give several clues until your listener(s) can determine what happened next. This can be done whether the book really is a mystery or not.

Mime: Become one of the characters from the story. Mime the most important events in your life. Practice in front of a mirror until you think your audience will understand your message.

Mime Team: Mime a scene or an important dialogue from the book with a friend or a group of friends. Be sure to include some of the highlights of the story. This is a great opportunity to communicate the feelings of different characters in the book.

Become the Author: Pretend you are the author. Appear on a TV or radio talk show to promote your book. Remember to share why you wrote this book and why you believe it is so important for people to read it.

Dramatic Reading: Choose the most exciting, suspenseful, dramatic excerpts from the book and practice reading them with a lot of feeling and expression. When you have it down, present your dramatic reading to an audience (your family, friends, grandparents, neighbors, or mom). This makes a great cassette tape!

Recitation: If the book has several selections, as opposed to one story, you might choose one poem, song, verse, or short story and recite it. Just as in the dramatic reading, use as much expression as you can muster. Now your hands will be free to use gestures!

Map: Create a large map (to scale if enough detail is given in the book) of the setting. Include terrain, locations of events, homes of characters, travel routes, geological features, etc. Be sure to include a legend.

Re-Publish It: Design a new book jacket . . . cover to cover. Illustrate it. Write about the author and the illustrator, of course. Include a mouth-watering scene on the back to entice the reader to read on...!

Postcards: Create a variety of postcards one or more of the characters might mail. Consider who they would write to and what they would write about. Use the details about the setting as described in the book to create your postcard set. After you design them, write to friends about your experiences as a character in the story.

Souvenirs: In addition to postcards, what other souvenirs might travelers through your story be interested in acquiring. Create a few. Present your "Souvenir Boutique" to an audience explaining what memories the souvenir owner might carry with each piece.

Cooking and Baking: Cook or bake some of the foods mentioned in the story. Share them with family and friends. Share your recipe, the steps you went through in the cooking process, and how these foods were used in the story.

Prepare a Meal: Plan, prepare, and serve a meal from the book. If there aren't enough foods mentioned for a complete meal, research the time period and location to discover additional foods that characters in the story may have eaten. At your meal, share why these foods were used in this time and place, and how and why they were prepared in this fashion.

Extravaganza: This event can be as extravagant as you wish. Use as many of the ideas presented here as you can. Add a few of your own. If several of you have read the same book, you will have even more to offer this occasion. Consider cooking and baking foods from the story or time period, dressing in costume, decorating according to a scene in the story, and displaying projects related to your book. You could create invitations based on the setting or characters. Prepare a presentation for your guests and present it at the extravaganza. Use your imagination. The sky is the limit!

SAMPLE APPROVED BOOK LIST

BOOK TITLE	AUTHOR	POINT VALUE
ANY CHRONICLES OF NARNIA BOOKS	C.S .LEWIS	15 PER BOOK (LIMIT 2)
HENRY REED'S BABY-SITTING SERVICE	KEITH ROBERTSON	10
ISLAND OF THE BLUE DOLPHINS	SCOTT O'DELL	15
SWISS FAMILY ROBINSON	JOHANN DAVID WYSS	25
ALICE IN WONDERLAND	LEWIS CARROLL	10
CADDIE WOODLAWN	CAROL RYRIE BRINK	15
THE STORY OF MY LIFE	HELEN KELLER	10
A CHRISTMAS CAROL	CHARLES DICKENS	15
LITTLE HOUSE BOOKS	LAURA INGALLS WILDER	15 PER BOOK (LIMIT 2)
NANCY DREW BOOKS	CAROLYN KEENE	10 PER BOOK (LIMIT 2)
BRIDGE TO TERABITHIA	KATHERINE PATERSON	10

GRADING SCHEDULE:
POINTS = A 50
POINTS = B 40
POINTS = C 30
POINTS = D 20

For some students, this grading schedule is sufficient to give a grade for reading or literature, for others it would be still more helpful to present a more complete picture for average reading points with project points to determine the student's grade.

Reading Genres

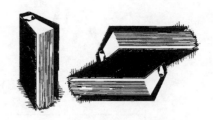

Genre	Type of Literature
Allegory	Characters or elements are symbols or representations.
Biography	True stories of people's lives. Includes autobiography.
Essays and Editorials	Author's opinion.
Fantasy	Stories of impossible situations, characters, magic, etc.
Historical Fiction	Based on true history and realistically set in an era.
Instruction	"How To."
News	Current events. Factual information.
Novels	Fiction—realistic or idealized.
Parables and Fables	Illustrations of a lesson or truth.
Plays	Story is told entirely through dialogue and intended to be acted out.
Poetry	Many forms exist to elegantly express thoughts and ideas.
Propaganda	Facts are mixed with opinion in order to persuade a targeted audience.
Reference Books	Facts arranged in a sequence for easy location or reference.
Reviews	Critique, generally of the arts.
Science Fiction	Situations that, based on science, may appear possible in the future.
Short Stories	Able to be read in a sitting.
Texts	Information organized into a logical scope and sequence.
Travel	Descriptive sketches of various travels.

Reading Genres

Name _THE MOON FAMILY_ _1998 - 1999 SCHOOL YEAR_

Objective _To read books from each of eight different_
genres this year as a family.

Genre	Date Completed	Title	Date Completed	Title
Allegory	1/31	PILGRIM'S PROGRESS		
Biography	9/15	BEN FRANKLIN	2/28	Thomas Edison
Essays and Editorials	WEEKLY	NEWSPAPER		
Fantasy				
Historical Fiction	11/14	THEE HANNAH		
Instruction	WEEKLY	PROVERBS		
News	WEEKLY	GOD'S WORLD		
Novels				
Parables and Fables	DAILY	BIBLE		
Plays				
Poetry	MONTHLY	BOOK OF VIRTUES	Monthly	Children's Book of Verse
Propaganda				
Reference Books	ONGOING	SEE REF .LIST		
Reviews	10/22	LISTEN MAG.		
Science Fiction				
Short Stories	MONTHLY	BOOK OF VIRTUES		
Texts	3/30	LIGHT AND GLORY		
Travel				

INDEPENDENT READING CONTRACT

Choose projects from "Book Project Ideas" to assign for books to be read during the quarter/semester/year.

APPROVED BOOKS & PROJECTS

SAMPLE

BOOK TITLE, AUTHOR	PROJECT/DUE DATE
LITTLE HOUSE IN THE BIG WOODS, LAURA INGALLS WILDER	INTERVIEW MIME MOBILE DUE—9/29
HELEN KELLER, THE STORY OF MY LIFE, HELEN KELLER	DRAMATIC READING RENT MOVIE, WRITE COMPARISON DUE—OCT 27
ASSORTED POEMS FROM *THE BOOK OF VIRTUES*, WILLIAM J. BENNETT	COLLAGE SONG, (PUT ONE TO MUSIC) WRITE ORIGINAL POEM DUE—11/17
A CHRISTMAS CAROL, CHARLES DICKENS	NEWS ARTICLE NARRATION DUE—12/15
CADDIE WOODLAWN, CAROL RYRIE BRINK	ILLUSTRATE SETTING ADD-A-CHARACTER RESEARCH AUTHOR, SETTING, TIME PERIOD DUE—JAN 26

STUDENT SIGNATURE/DATE *John M. Smith 9/6/99*

PARENT/TEACHER SIGNATURE/DATE *Mom Smith 9/6/99*

BOOK PROJECTS

(Teacher's Note: Choose projects from the "Book Project Ideas" section that seem appropriate for the literature selected and the student's abilities.)

Student's Note: The following book projects have been assigned point values based upon completing them in a manner that demonstrates your highest level of creativity, skills, and abilities. Anything less than your best effort will result in point deductions.

PROJECTS	BOOK *CADDIE WOODLAWN*		
PROJECT DESCRIPTION:	DATE DUE	POINTS POSSIBLE	POINTS EARNED
ILLUSTRATE SETTING IN 3-DIMENSIONS	*1-5*	*25*	*25*
INTERVIEW CADDIE'S MOTHER, WRITE OUT ALL QUESTIONS AND ANSWERS	*1-12*	*25*	*22*
WRITE A RESEARCH PAPER, INCLUDE INFORMATION ON AUTHOR, TIME PERIOD, CULTURE (two pp.)	*1-18*	*25*	*20*
DRAMATIC READING	*1-25*	*25*	*25*

SAMPLE

GRADING PERIOD: *2ND QUARTER*

GRADING SCHEDULE:
95 POINTS = A
85 POINTS = B
78 POINTS = C
73 POINTS = D

TOTAL POINTS EARNED: **92**

GRADE EARNED: **B**

Literature Project

Name *Jenny*   Book Title *Misty of Chicoteague*

Date Due   *Oct. 31, 8:30 a.m.*

Item	Points Possible/ Earned
* Read your book.	10 /*10*
* Record book title, author, illustrator, number of pages, and a brief summary of the story line on one page.	10 /*10*
Create a collage of highlights, symbols, settings, and important features of the story.	15 /*15*
Illustrate your favorite scene from the book. Incorporate as many details as possible.	15 /*13*
Pretend you are the main character in your story. Write a letter to someone telling about an important day or event in your life.	20 /*15*
Design a poster that would encourage people to read your book (like a poster advertising a movie that's just coming to the theater).	15 /
Choose the most exciting, suspenseful, or dramatic excerpt from the book to read aloud to family or friends. Practice reading with as much feeling and expression as you can.	20 / *18*
Cook or bake a special food mentioned in the story. Write about your experience.	20 /
Design a postcard that one of the characters in the story might send to someone he/she knows. Draw a scene on the front and write on the back.	20 /
Dress up like one of the characters in the story. Prepare to give a two to three-minute presentation about yourself including important information from the story.	30 /*26*
TOTAL POINTS EARNED	*107*

SAMPLE

Math Skills Checklist

Student Name *Jonathan*   Evaluation Period *1998-99*

Level *Grade 4 from Scope & Sequence*

Concept or Skill	Introduced	Practicing	Mastered	Not Addressed
Identify place value up to seven numbers			✓	
Read and write numbers with seven digits				
Whole number + and -			✓	
Two-digit x three-digit multiplication			✓	
Round & estimate multiplication			✓	
Round & estimate division		✓		
Division with two-digit divisor			✓	
Division with remainders			✓	
Addition of fractions with like denominators		✓		
Create equivalent fractions		✓		
Identify greatest common factor	✓			
Identify least common multiple				
Simplify fractions				
Write time to nearest minute				
Perform operations with money; make change				
Perimeter				
Identify lines, segments, cubes, pyramids				
Construct bar graph				
Solve two-step word problems				

The tendency is often to establish a goal of working straight through the student text. While there is nothing wrong with that goal, you could be leaving some gaps in your child's education. He may struggle along without ever understanding how to simplify fractions and his homework scores may not be too bad.

If, however, you create a scope and sequence checklist of the specific skills the student needs to demonstrate, such as the one on this page, it will become obvious where there are gaps. You will have the opportunity to address them nearer the time they are expected to be mastered and before you and your student become frustrated with even more complex skills.

EVALUATE

...to find the value or worth after study

"How did we do?"

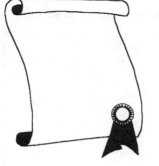

e-val´-u-ate: to find the value or worth after study

"How did we do?"

So, *how did you do*? Now that you have diagnosed, planned, and guided your students for some time, you are ready to evaluate the progress you have made. If you did a good job of planning, it should be fairly simple to assess whether or not you are meeting your goals. Some of the checklists and goals you have developed will double as evaluation tools now.

The following tools are provided as samples of evaluation methods. There are many more available to you through bookstores, testing services, curriculum fairs, and workshops. Keep in mind the most effective forms of evaluation are those which evaluate progress that you, the teacher, have planned and guided the student toward.

Once you evaluate, you have a new diagnosis from which to project and guide the student. Enjoy learning how to make evaluation a natural part of every area of the curriculum.

Tools to Evaluate

Portfolio

As the following pages explain, the portfolio shows *real* progress in the development of skills. Using the tools in this book as you create a portfolio also helps you determine if students are presenting their *best* efforts when they complete projects or assignments. The portfolio is helpful both in *evaluating* student progress and in *diagnosing* areas of need and accomplishment in order to plan the next goals and objectives.

Rubric

These lists help us differentiate between skills that have been mastered and those that need more work. The rubric enables us to do more than simply check off that skills have been addressed or mastered. It helps you, the teacher, judge the quality of performance within each skill area. The "Diagnostic Reading Checklist" and the "Diagnostic Writing Checklist," both included in the first section of this book, are examples of using a rubric. The same rubric can be used both to diagnose needs and readiness and to assess progress.

Mastery

Using a curriculum that teaches for mastery is another way to give students guidelines for achievement. The students know that when they demonstrate mastery at one level they move on to the next level. Step-by-step instructions are included. It is clear that when they began the year at level 18, and they are now at level 24, they have made progress. *SRA*, *Alpha-Omega*, and *Christian Light* are a few examples of mastery curriculum. See the "Mastery Math Chart" and the "Writing Mechanics and Punctuation" form as examples of developing tools for tracking mastery.

Critique

This extension of diagnosing by observation is especially helpful in creative subject areas such as reading, speaking, and visual and performing arts. You might use an audio or video recorder to capture an initial presentation. Observe and critique the presentation together with your student and put in writing what aspects need improvement. Later observe the next presentation and compare against the written critique.

Grading Schedule

The most objective way to see that material has been mastered is to calculate a percentage of the quality and quantity of work completed and assign a grade. It is not appropriate for every student or every subject, but it is simple to implement. Determine a number of points or a percentage on test scores or assignments that is necessary to receive a particular grade. For example: 92%+ = A, 85-91% = B, 76-84% = C...If a D or an F are not acceptable grades in your family don't even include them on the schedule. This is commonly used for math; however, the "Book Projects," "Writing Critique," and "Public Speaking Grading Schedule" are examples of using a grading schedule in other academic areas as well.

Portfolio Assessment

A portfolio is *a purposeful collection of a student's work* over the course of a term, a year, or several years, and is designed to paint as rich a picture as possible of that student's efforts, accomplishments, developmental levels in different areas, individual talents, strengths, and needs.

Students as well as parent/teachers should have a role in selecting work samples to be included and should be encouraged as frequently as possible to evaluate their learning both formally and informally. Student self-evaluations can become a valuable part of the portfolio.

The portfolio is an attempt to provide real knowledge about a student, his thinking, learning behaviors, attitudes, and performance that standardized tests cannot and do not give. While this information might not be as quantifiable as standardized test scores that can be translated into numbers and placed on graphs, it provides the very information that allows parents/teachers to know and reflect upon their students to plan for effective teaching. It is the full and rich picture that helps parents understand their child's unique abilities and needs. It is a completely individual representation of student efforts that provides students themselves with a basis for reflection, goal setting, and taking responsibility for their own teaching and learning as they mature.

Portfolios are an invaluable profile for future years of planning and teaching. They not only demonstrate a child's end-of-the-year levels of operation in each area of the curriculum but give insight into the rate and nature of growth those levels represented for that child in the previous year or years.

Consider the following reasons for using a portfolio to track student progress:

- To help you decide how much of your student's work to save and where to put it.
- To provide a consistent method of tracking student progress.
- To maintain a ready file of student work in any given subject, should you ever be asked "What do your kids do all day, anyway?"
- To use a more accurate measurement of student progress than A, B, C grading. For example, it was clear to see that in September your son could not write a complete sentence and he is now writing in complete paragraphs.
- To help your students observe their own progress when work is placed side-by-side.
- To develop good habits which will help students later in their academic life. Many colleges are weighing academic portfolios as heavily as transcripts and achievement test scores for new applicants.
- To provide you with ongoing objectives for student progress. Reviewing your student's portfolio gives you a great lesson plan. You can always see strengths and weaknesses. You can praise them for using their strengths, then develop a plan for building and improving skills that are weak or nonexistent.

Creating a Portfolio

There are a number of ways to establish a student portfolio. Any method of consistently collecting student work in the various areas of his/her studies can be considered a portfolio. This may be stored in a cupboard, a drawer, a filing cabinet or a cardboard box. The way you choose to set it up will depend upon what *you* plan to use it for and how readily available or transportable you wish it to be.

One of the simplest ways to create a portfolio is to set up a three-ring binder with sections for each subject included in the course of study. Additional areas of study or interest may be added as well. Select pieces of student work which represent skills and abilities for each subject area at the beginning of the school year. As students complete assignments or projects they are particularly proud of they should be encouraged to include these in their portfolios.

You will need to make some decisions about how the portfolio will be maintained and what will be included. This also will depend largely on *your* purpose for keeping the portfolio. What will be the criteria for selecting items to include in the portfolio? Do you wish to use the portfolio to collect a variety of student work or to show only the student's best work? Will you keep both diagnostic samples (pre-instruction) and final samples of work (after instruction in a specific skill area)? Will the portfolio only contain finished work? Might you or your student choose to keep unfinished projects in the portfolio as well? There are no right or wrong answers to these questions. Your answers to them will help you clarify your purpose for using the portfolio as a tool for evaluating your student's skills and progress.

You might have a consistent schedule for selecting portfolio items: i.e., the last week of each month, the end of the quarter, or weekly if it suits your needs. You will need to determine whether the portfolio is to be *teacher-directed* (you, the parent/teacher, decides what will be included) or *student-directed* (the student decides what to include). A combination might be appropriate depending upon the ages and maturity levels of your students.

One system of tracking progress through the portfolio might be to include 1 or 2 completed projects, papers, or assignments per subject area every five weeks, or semi-quarterly. This would result in 2 to 4 entries per quarter, thus, 8 to 16 per year in any given subject area. Sometimes we set a limit for the number of items to be included for a given subject area. My students then can choose which items will be kept and which will be replaced with new samples. Remember, not *everything* needs to end up in the portfolio.

Depending upon the size and number of entries, you might choose an artist portfolio, available in most craft stores as well as art supply stores. You might also want to consider separate portfolios in which to store samples of work for different subjects. For example, core curriculum subjects might be kept in labeled sections of the same three-ring binder while keeping a separate binder for work in a major unit study.

Portfolios need not exclusively hold work that demonstrates academic improvement. My children's portfolios are much like a year book. I select many samples of their work that I feel will help to give me a well-balanced picture of their educational progress. They also have the freedom to include any work sample of which they are particularly proud. In addition, their portfolios include references to many nonacademic or extracurricular experiences as part of their overall education. The following list of suggestions is given to assist you in planning your student's portfolio.

Portfolio Samples

- Pre- and post-tests
- Diagnostic work samples
- Post instruction work samples
- Writing samples representing a variety of purposes for writing
- Poetry
- Book list: all books that are read during the course of the year
- Art work
- Musical compositions
- Personal selections of which they are especially proud (This includes almost any "perfect paper.")
- Copies of selected friendly letters or other "real" correspondence
- Book, movie, and field trip reviews
- Pictures of outings, work experiences, school projects in progress
- Awards and certificates from various organizations, classes, clubs
- Certificates of achievement (from me) for various areas of the academic curriculum
- Music recital programs
- Field trip brochures and other literature
- Written notes for oral presentations

My children like to create covers for the portfolios. These usually include their picture plus stamps, stickers or drawings that represent their interests for that year. In addition to 3-ring binders, my own children keep "special boxes" which contain anything that doesn't fit in the binder.

Do keep in mind where the portfolio might need to be shown. You might be required to present it to school officials for evaluation every year. If you plan on re-entering children in a traditional school in grades K - 8, the school might ask to see it. If you think the portfolio might be viewed by school officials, consider maintaining some sections separate from the main portfolio which might reveal personal family information

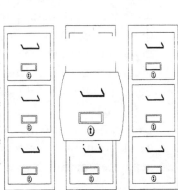

or a child's attitudes, values, and beliefs beyond those directly related to academic subjects.

Also keep in mind that school officials have very limited time to examine the portfolio, so, while you might keep eight to sixteen examples per subject per year, the school should receive only a portion of those.

For high school, the situation is much more complex. A portfolio serves as a supplement to a transcript which shows which subjects have been covered and the credits and grades earned. As Goals 2000 restructuring progresses, portfolios might be more readily accepted by public high schools and universities. Many private schools currently give portfolios significant consideration during the admissions and placement process.

On the following pages are samples that might be included in the student portfolio. In each of these scenarios only the parent/teacher can determine whether the progress made is consistent with the goals set. Either way it is obvious how much progress has been made and in how much time.

Portfolio Samples

1-9-96

William said everything about his jacket was in quite good condition except for the zipper.

Consider these penmanship samples. The first sample, done in January, demonstrates poor control of the pencil. The letters are not uniform in size or slant. Without a great deal of analysis you can see that this student's penmanship skills improved drastically over the next twelve months. The December 15 sample shows tremendous improvement in letter shape, size, and uniformity. Seeing these two samples placed side by side in his portfolio at the end of the year, this student remarked, "Mom, my handwriting got a lot better this year!" It's nice for our children to actually *see* themselves making progress.

12-15-96

William said everything about his jacket was in quite good condition except for the zipper.

Portfolio Samples

```
  2      4      2      4      8      9      8
  1      4      6      4      3      4      7
+ 4    + 1    + 2    + 4    + 6    + 5    + 4


 50     25     17     46     60     51     56
+ 42   + 21   + 32   + 12   + 28   + 41   + 43


 36     12     33     12     24     22     11
 43     14     22     12     62     22     35
+ 10   + 12   + 42   + 12   + 13   + 11   + 31


912     86    500            472    313
+ 67   +111   + 20   + 16
                       2-16-96
                       15 minutes
                       79%

800    222     .1     823    711    728
 72     33     23      34     33     50
+ 26   + 43   + 45   + 42   + 33   + 11


213    134    314    613    146    324
424    412    372    251    212    433
+262   +131   +312   +132   +320   +130
```

These two math samples demonstrate clear improvement in speed and accuracy in a relatively short time. In the first sample, done on February 16, the student took fifteen minutes to complete the drill with 79 percent accuracy. Less than one month later, on March 13, the same student took only six minutes to complete the drill with 100 percent accuracy.

```
  2      4      2      4      8      9      8
  1      4      6      4      3      4      7
+ 4    + 1    + 2    + 4    + 6    + 5    + 4


 50     25     17     46     60     51     56
+ 42   + 21   + 32   + 12   + 28   + 41   + 43


 36     12     33     12     24     22     11
 43     14     22     12     62     22     35
+ 10   + 12   + 42   + 12    3    + 11   + 31


912     86           323    472    313
+ 67   +111          + 56   + 20   + 16
              3-13-96
              6 minutes
              100%

800    222    111    823    711    728
 72     33     23     34     33     50
+ 26   + 43   + 45   + 42   + 33   + 11


213    134    314    613    146    324
424    412    372    251    212    433
+262   +131   +312   +132   +320   +130
```

Portfolio Samples

7-15-96

7-15-96 Writing Sample
It is important to learn
to read and write because...
When you grow & you dont now how
to read or write & you get a job beyond
to say this and you will not have
it veary long at all you will
before you know what happen to you.
You should be on streets being misera
-ble for rest of your life. Only you
can what tells you in the Bible.

Take a look at this first set of writing samples. This student is just learning about writing. His pre-instruction sample from July 15 contains poor sentence structure, a number of simple spelling errors, and not a lot of content. His post-instruction sample done five months later shows marked improvement in each of those areas.

12-10-96 Writing Sample
It is important to learn to read and write because if you grow up and can't read you won't understand Gods plans for you which are in the Bible. If you can't read, someone else has to read everything for you. This means you have to depend on others and they might not be trustworthy.

If you can't write you won't get a good job. It's important to be able to write so you can communicate with people. God says to record the things He has done so our children can read about them.

Reading and writing are especially important because they help you prosper and take good care of your family.

Portfolio Samples

This final set of writing samples also demonstrates a great deal of improvement. In the diagnostic sample done on August 1, the student does not demonstrate the ability to organize his ideas on paper. He has many errors in punctuation and some simple spelling errors as well. Nearly four months later, after instruction in proper essay format and a few lessons in punctuation, the same student completed a well-organized, clear and concise essay, complete with a topic sentence and a conclusion. This student compared the two papers in his portfolio and was very pleased with his own writing accomplishments.

8/1/96 *No Title?*
3rd draft

Topic Sentence?

    On July 14, 1789, a mob of Parisians attacked the Bastille Prison in the center of Paris. There were riots everywhere, and the government had gone broke. This was the begining of the French Revolution. When Louis sent troops to settle the matter, there were not enough, and the people revolted. The royal family tried to escape but were caught and imprisoned, and later tried and finaly executed in 1739.

Louis who?

meaning unclear

    In 1792 the people forced the king to sign a constitution, and built a small government, but it was still weak.

sentence? structure

    Also in 1792, Prussia and Austria attacked, but were driven out.

whom?

    In 1795 a Driectory of five men were elected, but the government was still very weak, and, despite the victories, the government was about to collapse.

was

    So in 1799 Napoleon I, a military hero, took over, and proclaimed himself emperor.

Conclusion?

An outline would have been helpful. What is your main idea?

Evolution or Creation?

Nathan 11/21/96

This paper is on evolution vs creation In it I will bring up several questions and theories based on evolution, and give the creationist's standpoint

In 1801, a French biologist, Jean Baptiste Lamark, proposed the first evolutional theory Lamark's theory had three points The first was *the theory of need* In order for an organism to evolve a structure it must need the structure The second was *the theory of use and disuse* If an organ was used by an organism, it would continue to evolve, if it was not, it would disappear The third was, *The theory of inheritance of acquired characteristics.* If an organism acquires a characteristic it can pass this characteristic on to its offspring All of these can be proved wrong in one example If a monkey used his tail we should "still" have long tails

Good point!

There are also many ways to prove the earth is young If the earth has been here for millions of years, there would be a lot more topsoil, and the major land masses would have eroded through rivers and streams into the oceans Take the Mississippi River for example There is so much silt coming down it that, at the present rate the entire delta could have accumulated in only 5,000 years!

The horse is often used as an example of evolution Evolutionists found an extinct animal that was the size of a terrier dog, with three toes on each hind foot They used it with many other "horses" in between to make a line of animals to show that evolution existed However, they do not have all the missing pieces and, therefore, cannot prove it The many animals they used for this theory had nothing to do with the theory they were trying to prove, which proves the theory wrong

Evolutionists think that since bird's wing bones look kind of the same as whale flippers, then they came from the same common ancestor In God's word we can clearly understand what is written when it says, "And God said, let the water be teeming with living creatures, and let birds fly above the earth across the expanse of the sky" It means a bird's wings were *created* to fly A whale's flippers were *created* to help him swim Therefore it is obvious that they did not come from the same ancestor, but were *created* by God individually

The ape to man theory is the evolutionist's idea of how man came to be Different people found different bone fragments in many different places They claimed that they were different parts of missing links that made up a line of animals that were our ancestors However, each one of the fragments was discovered to be part of a known animal This leaves only one conclusion: that man was *created* by God

Nice Conclusion!

The study of evolution shows many evolution stories that are all proved wrong by the great Creator The more we study evolution the more wrong it seems! We must try our very best to prove evolution wrong so that more people will understand and come to Christ I hope to use this study to show people that evolution is false religion, and that creation is fact!

Very well done! You followed directions & your content is well organized.

Portfolio Samples

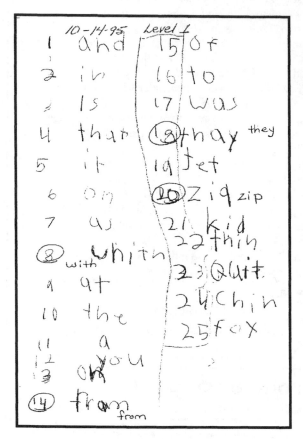

10-14-95   Level 1

1	and	15	of
2	in	16	to
3	is	17	was
4	than	18	thay *they*
5	it	19	Jet
6	on	20	Ziq *zip*
7	as	21	kid
8	whith *with*	22	thin
9	at	23	Quit
10	the	24	Chin
11	a	25	fox
12	OR *you*		
13			
14	fram *from*		

4-7-96   Level 4

1.	what.	14	peopele *people*
2.	were.	15	Water
3.	when.	16	Who
4.	your.	17	oil
5.	Said.	18	long
6.	Use	19	day
7.	which	20	down
8.	how	21	humber
9.	their	22	than
10.	if	23	Come
11.	other	24	made
12.	about	25	part
13.	Could		

These spelling tests speak for themselves. In October, this student was having difficulty with Level 1 in his spelling program. The following April he had only one mistake in Level 4.

Handwriting Critique

Student Name *Kenny*   Year *1998 - 99*

Handwriting Features *(Scale 1-5: 5=perfect)*	Assessment Date						
	9/5	10/10	12/6	1/7	2/22	4/25	6/7
Posture (back, feet, forearms are in proper position during writing)	1	4	5	3	5	5	5
Pencil Hold (pencil resting properly in relaxed hand)	1	4	5	4	5		5
Paper Position (student places paper in correct position for writing)	1	5				5	5
Stroke Direction (moves pencil in proper direction to form each letter)	2	3		3	5	5	5
Shape (each letter is formed correctly)	2	3	4	3	4	4	5
Size (properly sized in proportion to each other, upper and lowercase)	2	3	4	3	4	5	5
Slant (Slope) (varies with writing style, but should be consistent)	0	1	3	1	4	5	5
Spacing (proper spacing within and between words)	0	2	3	2	3	4	4
Speed (student maintains a consistent, comfortable rate of speed)	1	2	3	2	3	4	4
Height (tall and short letters begin and end where they should)	1	1	3	2	4	4	4
Consistency (consistent writing)	0	2	4	2	4	4	4
Overall Neatness and Legibility	1	3	4	3	4	4	4
Letters that need work next.	a,b,d, e,c,o	g,p,q	m,n, w	s,y,z	Caps	f,k,t, h	Caps

Note: Use with "Informal Handwriting Assessment" shown on page 35. Modify or add your own features based on a combination of your handwriting goals for the student and the next goals of the curriculum you are using.

Writing Mechanics and Punctuation

The "Writing Mechanics and Punctuation" chart shown on the next two pages might be used to evaluate the mechanics of writing within the context of any of the student's written work. The writing is reviewed and the progress recorded in numerical form so that it is measurable.

Remember, it may not be necessary to evaluate every piece of student writing for mechanics and/or punctuation. There are many reasons for writing; see the "Junior and Senior High Level Writing Assignments" list. You might ask your student to complete daily journaling assignments or note-taking exercises that are not corrected for spelling or punctuation. You might assign specific writing projects with an emphasis on mechanics and punctuation. Other assignments may emphasize content, form, or expression. Whatever your purpose, the more clearly you communicate it in advance, for yourself and your student, the simpler evaluation becomes.

You might use the "Writing Mechanics and Punctuation" chart as a diagnostic tool the first time. This will let you know which writing skills your student has already mastered and help you identify those which need instruction.

You may choose to evaluate mechanics of writing more or less often than this chart reflects, depending upon the student's writing ability and the skills and concepts being introduced. You could predetermine assessment dates at the beginning of a period of instruction, say at the beginning of the semester or the school year. You might decide you will give a writing assignment to be evaluated for mechanics and punctuation the first Friday of each month, or once every five weeks, etc. On the other hand, you could give a unit of instruction, for example in using commas, followed by an writing assessment. The next unit might focus on developing complete sentences, which should then be evident in a writing assessment.

A good rule of thumb for evaluating student work is that he will be held accountable for all the rules he has learned. In other words, if he knows the rules of spelling certain words, they should be spelled properly. If he has never been instructed, he should not be held accountable. It might be helpful to evaluate student writing for all of the mechanics and punctuation skills listed at the beginning of a new school year or term. After that, assessments might focus on the skills being addressed. Perhaps at the end of the year another comprehensive evaluation could be given.

It might be difficult at first for you to assign a number or some other very objective symbol to something as subjective as writing. In the long run such a system will enable you to measure progress and determine whether the method of instruction in writing skills is producing the desired results.

Writing Mechanics & Punctuation

Student Name *Nathan*   Year *1998 - 99*

Mechanics are evaluated within the context of written work that is reviewed on each of the assessment dates. You may choose to evaluate mechanics of writing more or less often depending upon the student's writing ability and the skills and concepts being introduced.

Skill	Assessment Date						
	9/5	10/10	12/6	1/7	2/22	4/25	6/7
Written Work Evaluated	Germany Report	The Hobbit Book Report	Essay: The Gospel	Essay: Founding Fathers	Crystal Project	Nutrition Research Paper	State Report
Mechanics:							
Capitals (20)	10 ·	13	14	14	16	18	17
Italics or Underlines:(5) ▪ Titles of books ▪ Proper names ▪ Foreign words and phrases ▪ Words named as words ▪ Emphasis	4	4	5	5	5	5	5
Abbreviations (5)	3	4	4	4		4	5
Numbers - Usage in writing (5)	4	4	5	5	5	5	5
Word Divisions: (5) ▪ Ends-beginnings of lines ▪ Compound words ▪ Hypenated words	3	4	5	5	5	5	5
Proper Verb Form: (20) ▪ Subject-verb agreement ▪ Past/present/future ▪ Singular/plural	13	15	15	16	15	18	17
Pronoun-Antecedent Agreement (10)	9	10	10	10	10	10	10
Complete Sentences (10) (no fragments or run-ons)	7	8	8	8	9	8	9
Proper Word Usage (20)	15	15	13	14	16	14	18
Paragraphs (10) ▪ Related sentences are grouped ▪ Indentations are used appropriately	8	8	7	8	9	10	9
Spelling (20)	6	9	15	16	18	15	18

Writing Mechanics & Punctuation, page 2

Skill	Assessment Date						
	9/5	10/10	12/6	1/7	2/22	4/25	6/7
Punctuation:							
End Punctuation: (20) ▪ Period ▪ Question mark ▪ Exclamation point	18	17	17	18	17	18	18
Commas: (20) ▪ Dates, addresses, place names, long numbers ▪ Introductory phrases and clauses ▪ Three or more items in a series ▪ With quotations ▪ To set apart phrases ▪ To set apart the person being addressed	12	14	14	12	17	18	17
Quotation Marks: (5)	3	4	5	4	5	4	5
Semicolon: (5) ▪ Long items in a series ▪ Joining main clauses ▪ Setting apart long main clauses	4	4	4	5	5	4	4
Apostrophes: (10) ▪ Possessives ▪ Contractions ▪ Plural possessives	6	6	7	8	7	8	8
▪ Other Punctuation: (10) ▪ Colon ▪ Dash, hyphen, slash ▪ Parentheses, brackets ▪ Ellipsis mark (. . .)	8	8	7	8	9	8	9
Total Points for This Writing Assessment Percentage Score (Divide total points by 200) *(Can be translated into letter grade.)*	133 67%	147 74%	155 78%	160 80%	173 87%	172 86%	179 90%

Note: 200 points possible. Deduct one point for each error in the appropriate category as you evaluate the student's written work. This student received a score of six for the first assessment in spelling. This means there were fourteen spelling errors in this paper.

If a writing feature does not apply, omit the category. For example, if the student does not yet use any of the "other punctuation," omit the category and adjust the points accordingly. You may add points to another category or simply account for the difference when you average the score. If you are placing a great deal of emphasis on a specific writing skill such as use of dialogue in a story, you might choose to give it more weight as there will be more opportunity for error in the student's work. You might deduct two points per error for a skill that was just taught to give it more attention, as well.

Charts like these are intended to take the guesswork out of evaluating writing.

WRITING CRITIQUE

Attach to all written assignments.

SAMPLE

Name *Suzy Q*   Due Date and Time *Oct 3/9:00 a.m.*
Title *John Sutter: An Early Californian*
Actual Completion Date and Time   *Oct 3/10:30 a.m.*

	POINTS POSSIBLE	POINTS RECEIVED
PROMPTNESS	10	8
NEATNESS	10	10
CONTENT (information)	20	17
EXPRESSION (vocabulary, description...)	20	18
MECHANICS (punctuation)	20	15
GRAPHICS (cover/charts/illustrations)	20	20
TOTAL POINTS RECEIVED	100	90
EXTRA CREDIT	+	5 *Nice Cover Design*
FINAL POINTS		92

GRADE: *A -*

CRITIQUE: *Nicely Done! We spent a lot of time discussing his personal life. It would have been nice if you had included more of it in your paper. Otherwise, you followed directions well and did a very thorough job.*

Public Speaking Evaluation

Individual Presentation

This form may be used to evaluate an oral presentation in any area of the curriculum.

Name *Loria*	**Topic/Title** *Why You Should Be Involved in Community Service*
Components of the Speech	Points Possible/Given
Detail	(10) / 9
Organization	(10) / 6
Poise	(10) / 9
Preparation	(10) / 8
Eye contact	(10) / 7
Articulation	(10) / 9
Expression	(10) / 7
Persuasiveness	(20) / 18
Beginning and ending with confidence	(10) / 10
Total Points Earned	83

Grading Scale:

90% = A

80% = B

70% = C

Below 70% you must repeat assignment.

Grade: *B*

Comments: *Your beginning and ending were very strong. Nice use of interesting details to draw us in. A little more practice would have allowed you to have more eye contact and to be more expressive. Tip—Memorize key quotes.*

Public Speaking Course Evaluation

Name _Stuart George_

This chart is shown as an example of establishing guidelines and expectations for a course of study in advance. Clearly laid out expectations make evaluation of even subjective disciplines such as oral presentations or writing much simpler. Use with "Public Speaking Evaluation for Individual Presentations" found in this section.

Effort	Oct. 2	Oct. 9	Oct. 16	Oct. 23	Nov. 6	Nov. 13	Nov. 14	Total Points
Assignments completed promptly	x	x	x	~1	x	x	x	9
Discussion	x	x	x	x	x	x	x	15
Respect shown parent/instructor	x	x	x	x	x	x	x	15
Shows ability to give & receive constructive comments	x	x		~2	x	x	x	13
Encouragement of other students (siblings apply)	x	x	x	~2	x	x	x	13
Preparation for presentations/discussions	x	x	x	~3	x	x	x	12
Following directions	x	x	x	~3	x	x	x	12
								89
Achievement								
Humor	100							100
Reading/Recitation		100		*100				200
Impromptu			92		*94		*96	282
Expository speech w/visual aids				72				72
Extemporaneous speaking					94			94
Persuasive speaking						93		93
Public speaking quiz						100		100
Dramatic/humorous interpretation							88	88
Final presentation								200
Total Points								1229

* = Extra Credit   Effort Grade = _89_   points = _B+_   Achievement Grade = _1229_   points = _A+_

RESEARCH PROJECT EVALUATION

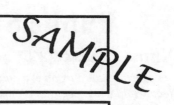

Name *Mary*   Due Date/Time *Jan. 8, 9:00 a.m.*

Project Name *Care and Keeping of Horses*

Actual Completion Date/Time *Jan. 8, 5:00 p.m.*

	POINTS POSSIBLE	POINTS RECEIVED
PROMPTNESS	10	8
NEATNESS	10	9
CONTENT (information)	20	18
EXPRESSION (vocabulary, description . . .)	20	16
MECHANICS (punctuation)	10	15
GRAPHICS (cover/charts/illustrations)	20	10
BIBLIOGRAPHY (references and format)	10	8
EXTRA CREDIT	10	0
FINAL POINTS	110	84
GRADE EARNED		B

GRADING SCALE:

93 points = A
90 points = A-
87 points = B+
83 points = B
80 points = B-

COMMENTS: *Your illustrations were very nice. Report was well laid out. We need to review punctuation rules. It would have been a good idea to do the extra credit. A rough draft would help.*

Geography Unit Study

This sample syllabus is based on Rea Berg's *Literature Approach to Geography* available from Beautiful Feet Books. The same format could be applied to any nontraditional or nontextbook approach to an area of study. The purpose is to break the course into small measureable units so the student's performance can be evaluated. Whether the reading and activities are completed in a class or group session, or the student is expected to work independently, the same method of evaluation can apply.

Activity	Method of Evaluation	Points Received
Read *Paddle-to-the-Sea*. (10)	Discussion	10
Research Report on Canadian geese. Follow Content Guidelines. (10)	Format Guidelines	(90%) 9
Glossary. (25) Select and define twenty-five words as you read through the book.	SAMPLE	25
Essay. Compare & Contrast the characteristics of a marsh and a pond. (20)	Writing Critique	(90%) 18
Research Paper—Discuss both the iron ore and copper industries. (15)	Writing Mechanics & Punctuation Evaluation	(85%) 13
Write a biography. Choose either Jacques Cartier or Samuel Champlain. (20)	Format Guidelines	(95%) 19
Point Subtotal	Average Points	94
Oral Presentation: Use the map to narrate the story of *Paddle-to-the-Sea* to our family.	Oral Presentation Critique	95
Map: labeled and colored. See Map Guidelines for details. (100)	Map Guidelines	94
Total Score	(Average Point Subtotal, Oral Presentation & Map Scores)	94% = A

Map Guidelines Label & color the following features on your map as you read through _Paddle-to-the-Sea._	Points Received
Canada (2)	2
Lake Nipigon, Lake Superior (4)	4
Isle Royal (2)	2
Duluth, MN; Superior, WI (4)	4
Minnesota, Wisconsin, Michigan, Illinois, and their capitals (6)	6
Apostle Islands; Keweenaw Peninsula (4)	3
Mark the location of the shipwreck (2)	2
Sault Ste. Marie (2)	2
Chart Paddle's course around Whitefish Bay (8)	7
Lake Michigan, Lake St. Clair (4)	4
Gary, Indiana; Chicago, Illinois (2)	2
Bay City, Detroit, Ontario (3)	3
Lake Huron, Lake Erie, Lake Ontario (6)	5
Ohio, Pennsylvania, New York, and their capitals (6)	5
Toledo, Sandusky; Cleveland & Astabula Ohio (4)	4
Erie, Pennsylvania; Buffalo, New York (2)	2
Niagara Falls. Draw a small depiction and paste on map (5)	5
Draw in the Welland Canal (5)	5
Toronto, Kingston, Thousand Islands (3)	3
St. Lawrence River, Lake Champlain, Gulf of St. Lawrence (6)	5
Montreal, Ottawa, Quebec (2)	2
Vermont, New Hampshire, Maine, and their capitals (6)	6
Portland, Maine; New York, New York (2)	2
Washington, D.C. (1)	1
Atlantic Ocean (1)	1
New Jersey, Connecticut, Massachusetts, Rhode Island and their capitals (8)	7
Total Map Score	94

Poetry Reading/Recitation Evaluation

Use this rubric for evaluating any oral reading or recitation, including Scripture memorization, poetry, short story, or family read-aloud time. This is easy for students to use to evaluate themselves and each other.

SAMPLE

Name ___Jeffrey___   Date ___1/16___

Beginning with Confidence (Poise)   1   2   ③   4   5

Pronouncing Words Well (Articulation and Enunciation)   1   2   3   ④   5

Volume   1   2   3   4   ⑤

Eye Contact   1   2   ③   4   5

Expression   1   2   3   ④   5

Total Points Earned ___19___

Poetry Reading/Recitation Evaluation

Name ___Jeffrey___   Date ___3/21___

Beginning with Confidence (Poise)   1   2   3   4   ⑤

Pronouncing Words Well (Articulation and Enunciation)   1   2   3   ④   5

Volume   1   2   3   ④   5

Eye Contact   1   2   3   4   ⑤

Expression   1   2   3   ④   5

Total Points Earned ___22___

SCIENCE PROJECT EVALUATION

Student's Name __NICHOLAS__   Year in School __8TH GR.__

	1	2	3	4	5
Originality and Creativity Idea, approach, and method show original and creative thinking.	1	2	3	4	(5)
Scientific Thought Knowledge of the subject of study is demonstrated, and scientific accuracy is evident.	1	2	3	(4)	5
Work and Organization Project indicates thought, time, and care in preparation and organization.	1	2	3	(4)	5
Visual Presentation Exhibit is neat and attractive. Project is clearly and thoroughly presented.	1	2	3	4	(5)
Oral Presentation Project is clearly explained to the evaluator.	1	2	3	4	(5)
Total Points Earned	23				
Grade Earned	A -				

Project Name __CRYSTALS__

__3/8/99__

Grading Scale: 24 points = A

16 points = B-
14 points = C+
12 points = C
10 points = C-

Due Date

Math Basics Record

Name *Sam*   **Evaluation Period** *1998-99*

Must achieve 95 percent accuracy or better to move to next level.

	10 min	8 min	6 min	5 min	4 min	3 min	2 min	1 min
Addition Facts: 100 facts, single digit					95% 9/6	97% 9/10	100% 5/22	
Subtraction Facts: 100 facts, single digit		95% 9/14	96% 9/17	97% 9/20	97% 9/23	100% 9/30		
Addition Facts: 50 facts, two-digit (no re-grouping)		95% 10/3	97% 10/8	98% 10/12				
Subtraction Facts: 50 facts, two-digit (no re-grouping)		95% 10/16	95% 10/22	95% 10/30				
Addition Facts: 50 facts, two-digit (re-grouping)			97% 11/3	100% 11/6				
Subtraction Facts: 50 facts, two-digit, (re-grouping)		95% 11/16	95% 11/21	95% 12/1				
Multiplication Facts: to 5 x 5			100% 12/5	100% 12/6	100% 3/3			
Multiplication Facts: to 10 x 10		95% 1/8	95% 1/16	96% 1/22				
Multiplication Facts: to 12 x 12	95% 1/8	95% 1/10	95% 1/22	97% 1/30				
Division Facts: to 5		97% 2/3	95% 2/8	95% 2/18				
Division Facts: to 8	95% 2/3	95% 2/18	95% 2/26	95% 3/3				
Division Facts: to 10		95% 3/3	96% 3/10	95% 3/20				
Division Facts: to 12	95% 3/10	95% 3/27	96% 4/7	95% 4/17				
Fractions: +,- with like denominators				100% 2/10	100% 2/15			
Fractions: simplify	95% 2/12	95% 2/17	95% 2/22					
Fractions: +,- without common denominators	95% 3/16	95% 3/24	95% 4/4					
Fractions: multiply and reduce to lowest terms		95% 4/10	100% 4/22					
Fractions: divide								
Decimals: +,-,x,÷	95% 5/2	95% 5/15	95% 5/22					
Convert decimals to fractions								
Percentages: convert to fractions and decimals								

Many math text books will include drill and practice for these basic facts. Look for them in the test booklet or in the front or back of the student text. There are a number of programs available that focus on drilling math facts for mastery. Check your local teacher supply store or curriculum catalogs.

The student continues to take the same test (or format, i.e., # problems, type) to improve time and accuracy.

ARITHMETIC LESSONS RECORD

BOOK TITLE _Math 54_   STUDENT NAME _Wendell_
PUBLISHER _Saxon_   GRADING PERIOD _1st quarter_
LEVEL _4th grade_

LESSON #	DATE	TIME SPENT	% SCORE	LESSON #	DATE	TIME SPENT	% SCORE
1	9-5	55 min	100	18	9-29	45	87
2	9-6	60	97	19	10-		
3	9-7	55	93	20	10-		
4	9-8	50	97	21	10-4	45	80
5	9-11	45	93	22	10-5	40	80
6	9-12	50	93	23	10-6	40	83
7	9-13	45	100	24	10-9	35	77
8	9-14	50	93	25	10-10	35	77
9	9-15	50	97	26	10-11	35	73
10	9-18	45	93	27	10-12	35	77
11	9-19	50	97	28	10-13	45	93
12	9-20	65	100	29	10-16	45	97
13	9-21	50	93	30	10-17	40	93
14	9-25	50	93	31	10-18	35	90
15	9-26	45	87	32	10-19	35	90
16	9-27	45	87	33	10-20	40	93
17	9-28	45	83	34	10-23	40	97

SAMPLE

ARITHMETIC TEST SCORES RECORD

TEST #	DATE	TIME SPENT	% SCORE	TEST #	DATE	TIME SPENT	% SCORE
1	9-11	45	97				
2	9-18	50	100				
3	9-26	45	97				
4	10-3	45	93				
5	10-10	50	97				
6	10-17	45	93				
			AVERAGE				AVERAGE

SAMPLE

STUDENT NAME Wendell
GRADING PERIOD   1st qtr.
AVERAGE LESSON SCORE (%) 89.2%
 (Add all lesson scores and divide
  by the number of lessons)
AVERAGE TEST SCORE (%) 96.2%

AVERAGE OF LESSON
AND TEST SCORES 92.7%
GRADE A -
COMMENTS: It pays to take your time, doesn't it? Slow down and check
your work carefully.

REFERENCE MATERIALS

List all reference materials used during the school year in any subject area. Include any materials: books, magazines, newspapers, audio, video, etc. that were used for reference purposes.

STUDENT NAME *JONATHAN*   SCHOOL YEAR *1998-99*

TITLE	AUTHOR/ PUBLISHER	TITLE	AUTHOR/ PUBLISHER
WEBSTER'S 1828 DICTIONARY	NOAH WEBSTER	ZOOBOOKS	WILDLIFE EDUCATION, LTD.
STRONG'S CONCORDANCE	JAMES STRONG	NATIONAL GEOGRAPHIC	
KING JAMES BIBLE		SCHOLASTIC DICTIONARY OF AMER. ENGLISH	SCHOLASTIC, INC.
NIV BIBLE	ZONDERVAN	STUDENT HANDBOOK	SOUTHWESTERN
TELEPHONE DIRECTORY		THE CHRISTIAN HISTORY OF THE CONSTITUTION	F.A.C.E.
"NAPA REGISTER"		TEACHING & LEARNING AMERICA'S CHRISTIAN HISTORY	F.A.C.E.
WORLD BOOK ENCYCLOPEDIA		PICTORIAL ATLAS OF THE WORLD	OTTENHEIMER
WEBSTER'S THESAURUS	LANDOLL		
TRAVEL GUIDE USA	READER'S DIGEST		
IT'S A BIG WORLD ATLAS	TORMONT		

Putting It All Together

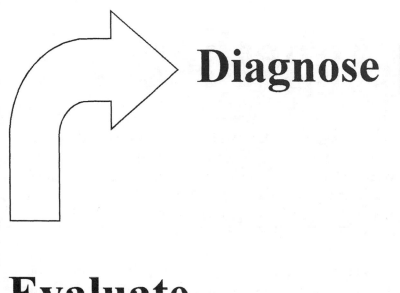

Diagnose

Plan

Evaluate

Guide

*"Now that I finally have it all together,
I can't remember where I put it."*

Putting It All Together

Now that you have learned how to **Diagnose, Plan, Guide,** and **Evaluate** your way through your child's educational program, it is time to put it all together. How will you use what you have learned? If you are a little bit overwhelmed at the moment, rest assured you are in good company. In most of my workshops, people leave feeling somewhat inundated with information, ideas, and especially with forms. Isn't it exciting that you have the opportunity to continue learning along with your children?

Remember, it is not necessary to use each and every form or sample offered in this book to teach and evaluate your children successfully. These are given as suggestions. They are some of the ways you can incorporate these four steps into your own educational program. Use those with which you are most comfortable. Start with one thing that makes sense and begin it now. You know the saying, "You can eat an elephant one bite at a time."

"A Place to Begin" is included to help you develop a step-by-step plan for using these materials. It is laid out in three levels, depending upon the grades/ages of your students. Also notice that the "Sample Forms Use Guide" demonstrates that most of these forms can be used several ways. Take a look at the "Oral Presentation Critique" to see how this works.

I've also added a section on critical thinking here because this is an area that overlaps all subject areas and all four steps of our planning and evaluation process.

The best thing about following these steps is that you can't fail. Even when you discover something is not working well, you have accomplished **evaluating** and **diagnosing** all over again. Now you are ready to **plan** new goals and **guide** yourself and your students toward them.

Suggestions for

Getting the Most out of this Book

📖   Decide you will use it. Haven't you invested in enough materials that are sitting on your shelf, collecting dust? Using this resource might help you recover some of them as well.

📖   Keep it in a convenient place. Put it with your lesson plans, on your kitchen counter, or in the middle of the school room table, anywhere you will see it often. For just a few dollars your local printer will three-hole punch it and you can keep it in your planning binder along with extra copies of the forms you use most often. I have a friend who posts her children's "Objective and Evaluation" forms on the wall in her dining room so she will refer to them daily.

📖   Find a buddy. "Two are better than one . . . for if either of them falls, the one will lift up his companion" (Eccl. 4:9-12). Get yourself an accountability partner, perhaps someone whose children are approximately the ages of yours, or someone who has been home schooling the same amount of time you have. Schedule times to pray together and hold one another accountable for making plans and sticking to them (maybe over the phone while the younger kids are napping).

📖   Share it with your local support group. The more the merrier! You will enjoy learning how your friends are incorporating these ideas. Sharing your diagnostic or evaluation ideas will encourage others and help you stay motivated to persevere.

📖   Set aside an afternoon or evening for children to share their "Book Projects," "Writing Assignments," or "Oral Presentations." Older students can fill out critiques for each other. They really enjoy this.

📖   Schedule family time for **Diagnosing, Planning, Guiding** and **Evaluating.** This way everyone gets to participate. Children especially love to have both Mom and Dad see how much they've progressed! (It adds a little pressure when they haven't done their share also.) Be sure to use this time to agree as a family on what is "of value" or "worth" in the educational program.

📖   Get your children on your team. This takes some initial planning, but in the long run it is well worth it. When I lay out goals and objectives with and for my children, they keep me on track. My children are quick to say, "Gee, Mom, I thought our family was going to get through these books this month. We'd better get going or we won't get finished when we're supposed to." It also helps when they know what's coming next. When they're anticipating the next project, book or unit study, they have a little more incentive for completing the one they're in.

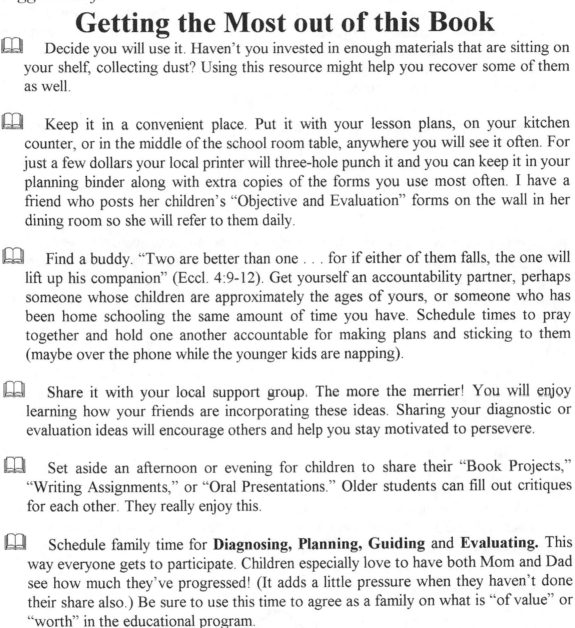

📖   Help your children set up their own record-keeping notebook. Many of the forms included in this book are appropriate for children to complete for themselves. Even older elementary grade students can keep track of their own math scores, literature projects, book contracts, physical education records, and portfolios. This is a great way to teach them responsibility. I tell my students if it isn't recorded, it doesn't count. They catch on very quickly.

📖   Require students to turn in the appropriate evaluation form with the assignment when it is due. This saves a lot of time when it comes to grading. I deduct points if they don't turn in the proper critique with a project. I tell them it's kind of like a time card or a billing statement. Some day they will have their own jobs and, without completing the proper paper work, they won't be paid.

📖   Ask students to complete their own critiques before you evaluate their work. They might surprise you. Sometimes they notice things that we overlook. This also causes them to pay attention to the details for which their work is being evaluated. It helps them make the connection between the grade and the actual merits of the work produced. This alone is a valuable skill.

📖   Have your student complete his own report card or progress report. Require him to substantiate his grades with evaluations and work samples from the term for which he is being graded. Compare his report card with the one you completed for him. Discuss the grades together. His perceptions of the progress he has made should help you guide him in the future. This is another great time for Mom and Dad to talk together with their student.

📖   Ask your students to develop a course outline, literature or science project, or book contract using forms from this book. They can select tasks and assign them point values. Of course, it must meet your approval before it actually becomes a real assignment. Your children will almost always support what they help to create. This gives them an added incentive to put forth their best effort and makes your job easier at the same time.

A Place to Begin

If your children are approximately pre-school through third grade (or about four to eight years of age) . . .

☐ Pray and ask the Holy Spirit to be *your* teacher.

☐ Complete the "Educator's Diagnostic Assessment." Use this information to help you with the "Educator's Objectives."

☐ Share your objectives with someone who will support you in fulfilling them.

☐ Complete the "Observation Notes." In doing so, watch your child at several different times of day over a period of several days.

☐ Complete both the "Diagnostic Reading" and "Diagnostic Writing" checklists.

☐ Have your student complete a handwriting sample. Use the "Handwriting Critique" to diagnose his current writing skills.

☐ Give your child either a pre- or post-test or a review page from his math curriculum.

☐ Set up your child's portfolio and add all of the above items to it.

☐ Read through the scope and sequence for your child's grade level. You might wish to use it as a checklist. The items that are not checked will be included in your objectives.

☐ Use all of these tools to lay out your child's "Individualized Educational Program (IEP)."

☐ Now you can set specific objectives on the "Objectives and Evaluation Form" for the coming quarter.

☐ You might enjoy taking the "Reading" and "Writing Inventory(ies)" together with your child.

☐ Set up an "Approved Book List."

☐ Keep your IEP and your "Objectives and Evaluation" forms in a place where you will refer to them regularly.

☐ Continue adding to the portfolio.

☐ Each time you use an Evaluation tool, math or spelling test, handwriting critique, etc., compare it to the last one. Be sure to point out your child's progress so he can see it too!

☐ Your last **Evaluation** has just become a new **Diagnosis**. Plan a new goal and guide your student toward it.

"Do not grow weary in doing good, for at the proper time we will reap a harvest, if we do not give up." Galatians 6:9

A Place to Begin . . . again

If your children are at approximately fourth through sixth grade levels . . .

☐ Pray and ask for the Holy Spirit to be *your* teacher.

☐ Complete the "Educator's Diagnostic Assessment." Use this information to help you with the "Educator's Objectives."

☐ Share your objectives with someone who will support you in fulfilling them.

☐ Complete the "Observation Notes." In doing so, watch your child at several different times of day over a period of several days.

☐ Give your student the "Student Reading Inventory" and the "Student Writing Inventory," as well as the "Student Inventory."

☐ Use the scope and sequence for your student's grade level as a checklist for skills mastered. Those that are not checked will be included in your objectives.

☐ Give your student a math test from your math curriculum.

☐ Have your student complete a handwriting sample.

☐ Use a "Writing Prompt" to get a sample of your student's writing.

☐ Give a "Critical Thinking Assignment" to diagnose your student's critical thinking skills.

☐ Put all of the above listed items in your student's portfolio.

☐ Use all of these tools to lay out your child's "Individualized Educational Program (IEP)."

☐ Now you can set specific objectives on the "Objectives and Evaluation Form" for the coming quarter.

☐ Go through each area of the curriculum that you have laid out and find a diagnostic tool to use, i.e., math drills, history pre-test, spelling final, physical fitness activities, etc. Keep all of these in the Portfolio so you can compare against them to measure progress.

☐ Set up an "Approved Book List." Begin your "Reference Materials List."

☐ Lay out a "Literature Project" or a "Book Contract."

☐ Set up your student's "Record-Keeping Notebook." Have him keep track of all his math lessons and tests, physical fitness, book contracts, and any student project timelines.

☐ Continue to refer to your "Objectives and Evaluation Form" so you will remember what you are working toward.

☐ Begin adding any additional areas you want included in your student's course of study. Develop a research project, unit study, science project or assign a series of oral presentations. There are forms included for each of these areas. Remember to give clear, specific, detailed directions for any project you assign.

☐ Continue adding to the portfolio. Each time you use an evaluation tool, math or spelling test, "Handwriting Critique," etc., compare it to the last one. Be sure to point out your child's progress so he can see it too!

☐ Your last **Evaluation** has just become a new **Diagnosis**. Plan a new goal and guide your student toward it.

"Do not grow weary in doing good, for at the proper time we will reap a harvest, if we do not give up." Galatians 6:9

A Place to Begin . . . again

If your children are in approximately seventh grade through high school . . .

☐ Pray and ask for the Holy Spirit to be *your* teacher.

☐ Complete the "Educator's Diagnostic Assessment." Use this information to help you with the "Educator's Objectives."

☐ Share your objectives with someone who will support you in fulfilling them.

☐ Find a good scope and sequence to use as a checklist for basic skills.

☐ In addition to reading this book, use *The High School Handbook*, by Mary Schofield and *Christian Home Educators' Curriculum Manual: Junior/Senior High*, by Cathy Duffy to help you plan a two- or four-year course of study for your junior or senior high student.

☐ Use a "Writing Prompt" to get a sample of your student's writing. Use the "Writing Mechanics and Punctuation" evaluation to critique the diagnostic writing sample.

☐ Give your student a math pre- or post-test from the math curriculum you have chosen. If you have not yet chosen a math curriculum, review the *Christian Home Educators' Curriculum Manual: Junior/Senior High* to assist you in making curriculum choices.

☐ Go through each area of the curriculum that you have laid out and find a diagnostic tool to use, i.e., math drills, history pre-test, spelling final, physical fitness activities, "Critical Thinking Assignment," etc. Keep all of these in the portfolio so you can compare later work against them to measure progress.

☐ Consider asking your student to complete his own "Observation Notes" and "Character Qualities Review."

☐ Use the above tools to assist you in laying out your child's IEP. I recommend doing this together with junior and senior high level students.

☐ Help your student begin setting up his portfolio. All of the above mentioned items should be included in it.

☐ Set up an "Approved Book List" and lay out "Literature Projects" or a "Book Contract."

☐ Help your student set up a "Record-Keeping Notebook." Have him keep track of all his math lessons and tests, "Physical Fitness Record," "Book Contracts," "Reference Materials" list, and any "Student Project Timelines." He should be able to tell you where he stands in a given subject any time you ask.

☐ Be sure that each project or assignment is given with an evaluation form or critique so that you and your student both know what is expected.

☐ Have your student develop a project or course outline using tools from the book for an area of study included in the IEP.

☐ Establish a schedule for evaluating progress and planning new goals at regular intervals together with your student.

"Do not grow weary in doing good, for at the proper time we will reap a harvest, if we do not give up." Galatians 6:9

Oral Presentation Critique

Name_____
Topic_____
Date Given_____

Components of the Speech	Points Possible /Given
Beginning with Confidence	(5)
Use of Interesting Details	(10)
Organization	(15)
Appropriate Use of Visual Aids	(10)
Poise	(10)
Preparation	(15)
Eye Contact	(10)
Articulation	(10)
Expression	(10)
Ending with Confidence	(5)
Total Points Earned	(100)
Comments:	

A Multipurpose Tool

This oral presentation critique presents an opportunity to use the same tool to **Diagnose, Plan, Guide,** and **Evaluate.**

The student gives a presentation and you, the parent/teacher, evaluate it using this simple critique. Your student then prepares a series of short presentations keeping these components of a well-constructed and well-delivered speech in mind. Continue discussing areas of progress and those which show improvement.

Each presentation provides the opportunity for:
✓ Further evaluation of progress
✓ Re-diagnosing the student's strengths and weaknesses
✓ Keeping the projected goals in front of both you and your student
✓ Guiding the student toward the goals of preparing and delivering a good oral presentation.

This list of components serves as a suggestion of how you might create your own tool. There is nothing set in stone about which components of an oral presentation are critical for a student to succeed at communicating with an audience. There are certain skills that are important to *you* for *your* children. Emphasize those which are most important to you. Some areas will become more important depending upon the topic or the nature of the presentation. Visual aids will not always apply and, in some instances, the organization of the content may need more emphasis than in others.

Sample Forms Use Guide

The following sample forms are listed in the order in which they appear in the book. Although each form is included in a particular section, i.e., **Diagnose***, it can have many uses. This chart is designed to help you consider ways to use the tools provided in this book. Refer to the samples for help in completing the forms you choose to use from the* **Appendix***.*

Sample Form	Diagnose	Plan	Guide	Evaluate
Educator's Diagnostic Survey	x	x		x
Suggested Scope and Sequence	x	x	x	x
Diagnostic Reading Checklist	x			x
Student Reading Inventory	x			x
Diagnostic Writing Checklist	x			x
Student Writing Inventory	x			x
Student Writing Sample	x			x
Observation Notes	x			
Informal Handwriting Assessment	x			x
Character Qualities Review	x	x	x	x
Student Inventory	x			x
Individualized Education Program (IEP)		x	x	
IEP Student Success Study Team	x	x		
IEP Annual Goals and Methods		x		
IEP Special Education	x	x		
Educator's Objectives		x	x	x
Objectives and Evaluation Form		x	x	x
Junior and Senior High Level Writing Assignments		x	x	x
Physical Education Record		x	x	x
Oral Presentation Student Guidelines			x	x
Format for One-page Essay			x	x
Sample Writing Assignment	x		x	x
Science Project Student Timeline		x	x	x
Student Project Timeline		x	x	x
Public Speaking Course Outline			x	x
Course Outline: Music			x	x
Approved Book List			x	x
Reading Genres		x	x	x
Independent Reading Contract			x	x

Sample Forms Use Guide

Sample Form	Diagnose	Plan	Guide	Evaluate
Book Projects			x	x
Literature Project			x	x
Math Skills Checklist		x	x	x
Handwriting Critique			x	x
Writing Mechanics and Punctuation		x	x	x
Writing Critique			x	x
Public Speaking Evaluation for Individual Presentations			x	x
Public Speaking Course Evaluation		x	x	x
Research Project Evaluation		x	x	x
Geography Unit Study			x	x
Map Guidelines			x	x
Poetry Reading/Recitation Evaluation	x		x	x
Science Project Evaluation		x	x	x
Math Basics Record			x	x
Arithmetic Lessons Record				x
Arithmetic Test Score Record				x
Reference Materials				x
Oral Presentation Critique	x	x	x	x
Critical Thinking Assignment	x	x	x	x

Assessing Critical Thinking Skills
Teaching Children to *Think*

What are "critical thinking skills" and why are they so important? Perhaps you have friends who think this is just a buzz-word today. Or, you might not have heard this title, but you have probably asked yourself how you can teach your children to *think*. What's the difference between thinking and critical thinking?

"Critical Thinking" has gone by several names in a variety of resources dealing with the discipline of the mind. Also referred to as "Higher Order Thinking Skills," "Logic," "Reasoning," and even at times "Values Clarification," critical thinking has taken a bad rap in recent years. The biggest reason for this is that parents are the only ones really qualified to teach their children to think critically. Why is that? To begin with, critical thinking, by any name, assumes taking a closer look at something and drawing conclusions based on fundamental beliefs and values. You can't make judgments unless you have a standard by which to judge.

Thus, it is imperative that we as parents assume the responsibility for teaching our children to think. To think critically does not necessarily mean to think judgmentally. It means training our children to do more than merely observe the world and ideas around them. They must be trained to also comprehend, evaluate, and apply the ideas they come across.

This section is designed to give you some tools for stretching your children to higher levels of thinking in every area of life and learning, however ordinary or complex. Though the concepts apply to both children and adults, the tasks chosen to train and evaluate thinking will differ according to the maturity of each person.

If this is a book about evaluating our children's progress, why are we discussing how to *teach* them something? The answer is simple. If you have been reading this far, you realize that in order to evaluate progress, we have to know what we are looking for. We must have a desired goal in mind. Therefore, in order to evaluate our children's ability to think, we must know what thinking looks like. This is not about motivating your child to think. Check out some good child-training materials, tapes, and seminars for that very important aspect of education. Instead, this is about clarifying what higher levels of thinking look like so we can aspire to them, recognize them when they occur, and make changes when they do not occur.

Several philosophers, psychologists, educators, and even clergy throughout history have attempted to describe and explain how people think and reason. Each has had his own system and terminology. For purposes of our clear understanding, I am going to use the following terms for describing levels of thinking.

Critical Thinking Skills...

Knowledge: The first level of thinking, knowledge is demonstrated when the student can recall facts or observations, or retell the story. Toddlers are capable of demonstrating this level of thinking. They look at the ball and say, "blue," or "ball," or "Sissy's." They have demonstrated knowledge. They might look in the picture book and point to the circle, square, mommy, elephant, etc. This is knowledge. Older students state facts from their reading or lecture. While it is necessary, it is the lowest level of thinking. Fill-in-the-blank and multiple choice exams usually test knowledge. Our students need to be stretched beyond knowledge.

Comprehension: This level of thinking requires understanding and using the information in your own words. Instead of retelling the story verbatim or restating the facts, the student needs to be able to summarize or paraphrase the information in discussion or writing.

Application: This third level of thinking expects the child to use the information in a new situation. It supposes questions such as, how does this apply to my life? How would my life be different if I used this information? What are all the possible uses for this product, material, etc.?

Analysis: Thinking is now becoming more abstract. This level of thinking requires separation into parts. The student must classify, dissect, categorize, compare, and contrast ideas and elements in order to analyze. Younger students can be helped to make the transition to this more abstract thinking by separating concrete objects into categories.

Synthesis: Creative students have been doing this for a long time. To synthesize something is to use it in a new way. When this level of thinking is achieved, the student is able to create, hypothesize, and invent new ways of using information and ideas. This is often expected in the study of science but can be applied to any area of the curriculum.

Evaluation: This is considered the highest level of thinking. It is the most abstract, yet it requires some absolute standard by which to judge, defend, or determine worth. This is the foundation of this book. By virtue of the fact that it is the highest level of thinking, it is also the most difficult to achieve. Many adults today do not know how to evaluate ideas, philosophies, situations, performance, etc. If we don't teach them how to evaluate and what is of worth, someone else will attempt to. If children don't ever learn to evaluate, someone else will do it for them. Somehow we have to teach our children to evaluate by an absolute standard. This is the stuff leaders are made of.

Trying Out Thinking Skills

This simple exercise may help you determine at what level your child is most comfortable thinking. Find an unidentifiable object. It needs to be something the child has not seen before and would not recognize in order to stretch him to higher levels of thinking. Place the object in the center of the table or in the middle of the room. Direct your child through the following exercises in the order given.

⌘ **Observe** this object. (Knowledge)
⌘ **Describe** this object. (Comprehension)
⌘ **List** all the possible uses you can think of for this object. (Application)
⌘ **Categorize** your uses into practical and impractical. (Analysis)
⌘ **Combine** any two uses for this object and invent a new item. (Synthesis)
⌘ **Decide** the best use for this object. Explain why this is the best use. (Evaluation)

If your child was able to carry out all of these tasks, he is capable of the highest levels of thinking. If your child could only go through **List**, you know he is capable of the first three levels and your next goal is to help him analyze the knowledge he is gaining. The older your child, the more you will expect.

As always, it will be helpful for you to record your observations as your child works through this exercise. If you ask him to respond in writing, save it in the portfolio for comparison at a later date.

If a child demonstrates the ability in this situation to think at the highest levels, it does not mean our job is finished. It is necessary to encourage children to stretch their thinking skills. It will help to have a plan for doing this. If you settle for **Knowledge** and **Comprehension,** so will your child. Have you noticed they often take the easy way out? The following pages include several tasks for challenging students to use each level of thinking.

Remember, it is not necessary to use the name **Critical Thinking** each time you are following this format. The types of questions, activities, and discussion on the following pages can be integrated into everything you and your children study and encounter.

Incorporating Critical Thinking into Your Curriculum
Or *Guiding* Your Students Through Critical Thinking

These words are designed to help you encourage your students to think critically in each area of the curriculum. Give them assignments orally or in writing that require them to carry out the activities listed under each level of thinking. Note the way these word lists are used to direct students through the activities on the following pages. Create your own or draw from the suggestions on the next few pages.

1. Knowledge
Direct students to:

recall	ask
observe	listen
read	name
state	retell

2. Comprehension
Ask students to:

identify	research
locate	restate
paraphrase	write
fill in	describe
summarize	explain

3. Application
Instruct students to:

sketch	construct
survey	use
simulate	apply
graph	list
draw	replicate
chart	make

4. Analysis
Tell students to:

classify	compare
dissect	categorize
advertise	separate
analyze	relate
contrast	breakdown
group	take apart

5. Synthesis
Teach students to:

design	create
invent	produce
pretend	hypothesize
add to	combine
suppose	compose

6. Evaluation
Guide students to:

judge	decide
determine	defend
debate	evaluate
establish worth	
grade	
appraise	

Critical Thinking Assignment

Name _Candace_   Date Assigned _12/7/98_ Date Due _1/15/99_

SAMPLE

Topic: _Automobile Air Bags_

Knowledge:
Read an article about the safety of air bags in automobiles.

Comprehension:
In your own words restate the way air bags work.

Application:
Graph some statistics you have uncovered about air bags.

Analysis:
Make an advertisement for air bags

Synthesis:
Design a different use for air bags (not in automobiles).

Evaluation:
Decide whether you would prefer to have air bags in your automobile or not. Defend your position.

Critical Thinking Tasks

These activities are designed to evaluate the way children think. Use them as models or create your own. Once they get the hang of it, your children will enjoy coming up with their own activity lists.

Topic: George Washington
Ask several people what they know about George Washington.
Research and **Write** a one-page report about his life.
Draw a picture of George Washington.
Compare and **Contrast** George Washington with Abraham Lincoln.
Create a short play about George Washington.
Determine which of his accomplishments is most important. **Defend** your **Decision**.

Topic: Rivers
Read a book about life near a river.
Research the river closest to you and write a one-page report about it.
List all the rivers in your state.
Compare two rivers and list all the similarities and differences you can find.
Decide if you would like to go rafting for a day. Which river would you raft down? Why?

Topic: Cartoons
Observe your favorite cartoon character.
Identify your cartoon's characteristics and list them.
Sketch a picture of your cartoon in pencil.
Advertise the comic strip by making a poster on newsprint, using markers.
Invent a character to befriend your favorite cartoon character.
Grade this comic strip with a rating between 1 and 10. **Defend** your rating.

Topic: Musical Style
Read about a musical composer.
Research the composer's musical style. **Describe** it in your own words.
Survey ten people. Ask for their opinions of the composer's musical style.
Listen to another composer's music. **Compare** and **Contrast** the two styles in writing.
Compose a musical arrangement similar in style to this composer's.
Judge the quality of your own composition. Upon what do you base your **Judgment?**

Topic: Periodic Table of the Elements
Observe the Periodic Table.
Locate copper on the table.
List the inert gases.
Categorize twelve elements a different way.
Invent a new element. Give it a name, atomic weight, and characteristics.

GLOSSARY OF TERMS

"An immense effect may be produced by small powers wisely and steadily directed."
Noah Webster, 1821

GLOSSARY OF TERMS

All definitions are taken from American Dictionary of the English Language,
Noah Webster, 1828.

ACCOMPLISH: To complete; to finish entirely. To execute; as to *accomplish* a vow. To gain; to obtain or effect by successful exertions; as to *accomplish* a purpose. To fulfill or bring to pass. To furnish with qualities which serve to render the mind or body complete, as with valuable endowments and elegant manners.

ACCOMPLISHING: Finishing; completing; fulfilling; executing; effecting; furnishing with valuable qualities.

ACHIEVE: To perform, or execute; to accomplish; to finish, or carry on to a final close. To gain or obtain, as the result of exertion.

APPRAISE: To set a value; to estimate the worth, particularly by persons appointed for the purpose.

APPRAISER: One who values.

APPRISE: To value; to set a value in pursuance of authority. It is generally used for the act of valuing by men appointed for the purpose, under direction of law, or by agreement of parties.

ASSESS: To set, fix, ascertain; to value; to fix the value of property (usually pertaining to taxation).

ASSESSMENT: A valuation made by authorized persons according to their discretion.

CRITIQUE: A critical examination of the merits of a performance; remarks or animadversions on beauties and faults. Science of criticism; standard or rules of judging of the merit of performances.

DEMONSTRATE: To show or prove to be certain; to exhibit.

DIAGNOSTIC: Comes from the Greek "to know."

EARN: To merit or deserve by labor or performance; to do that which entitles to a reward, whether the reward is received or not.

GLOSSARY OF TERMS

EDUCATION: The bringing up, as of a child; instruction; formation of manners. Education comprehends all that series of instruction and discipline which is intended to enlighten the understanding, correct the temper, and form the manners and habits of youth, and fit them for usefulness in their future stations. To give children a good *education* in manners, arts and science, is important; to give them a religious *education* is indispensable; and an immense responsibility rests on parents and guardians who neglect these duties.

EXECUTE: Literally to follow out or through. Hence, to perform; to do; to effect; to carry into complete effect; to complete; to finish. We *execute* a purpose, a plan, design or scheme; we *execute* a work undertaken, that is we pursue it to the end. To perform; to carry into effect. To perform what is required to give validity to a writing, as by signing and sealing.

GUIDE: To lead or direct in a way; to conduct in a course or path; to direct or order; to influence; to give direction to; to instruct; to regulate and manage.

KNOWLEDGE: A clear and certain perception of that which exists, or of truth and fact; learning, illumination of the mind; acquaintance with a fact or person.

LEARN: To gain knowledge of; to acquire knowledge or ideas of something before unknown. We *learn* the use of letters, the meaning of words and the principles of science. We *learn* things by instruction, by study, by experience, and by observation. It is much easier to *learn* what is right, than to *unlearn* what is wrong. To acquire skill in any thing; to gain by practice a faculty of performing; as, to *learn* to play a flute or an organ. To gain or receive knowledge; to receive instruction; to take patter; to receive information or intelligence.

OBSERVE: To see or behold with some attention; to notice. To take notice or cognizance of by the intellect. To utter or express, as a remark, opinion or sentiment; to remark. To keep religiously; to celebrate. To keep or adhere to in practice; to comply with; to obey; as, to observe the laws of the state. To practice. To be attentive.

PERFORMANCE: Execution or completion of any thing; a doing; as the *performance* of work or of an undertaking; the *performance* of duty.

PROGRESS: *noun.* A moving or going forward; a proceeding onward. A man makes a slow *progress* or a rapid progress on a journey. A moving forward in growth; increase. Advance in business of any kind. Advance in knowledge; intellectual or moral improvement; proficiency. The student is commended for his *progress* in learning; the Christian for his *progress* in virtue and piety. Passage from place to place. *verb.* To proceed. To continue onward in course. To advance; to make improvement.

GLOSSARY OF TERMS

PLAN: To arrange the parts of (design).

TEST: To compare with a standard; to try; to prove the truth or genuineness of any thing by experiment or by some fixed principle or standard; to refine gold or silver.

VALUE: *noun.* Worth; that property or those properties of a thing which render it useful or estimable; or the degree of that property or of such properties. The *real* value of a thing is its utility, its power or capacity of procuring or producing good. But there is, in many things, an *estimated* value, depending on opinion or fashion, such as the value of precious stones.
verb. To estimate the worth of; to rate at a certain price; to apprise; to have in high esteem; as a *valued* poem or picture. A man is apt to *value* his own performances at too high a rate; he is even disposed to *value* himself for his humility. To esteem; to hold in respect and estimation; as, to *value* one for his works or virtues. To take account of. To reckon or estimate with respect to number or power. To consider with respect to importance.

WISDOM: The right use or exercise of knowledge; the choice of laudable ends, and of the best means to accomplish them. This is wisdom in act, effect, or practice. If wisdom is to be considered as a faculty of the mind, it is the faculty of discerning or judging what is most just, proper and useful, and if it is to be considered as an acquirement, it is the knowledge and use of what is best, most just, most proper, most conducive to prosperity or happiness. Wisdom in the . . . practical sense is synonymous with discretion. It differs somewhat from prudence, in this respect; prudence is the exercise of sound judgment in avoiding evils; wisdom is the exercise of sound judgment either in avoiding evils or attempting good. Wisdom is true religion; godliness; piety; the knowledge and fear of God, and sincere and uniform obedience to his commands.

APPENDIX

Appendix

The following forms are provided for your use as a home school teacher and/or private tutor. They are intended to be reproduced for that purpose only. They have been placed at the back of this manual for your convenience.

Reproduction of these pages by the home school teacher or private tutor for use within the family is permissible. All other reproduction requires the prior written permission of the publisher.

Educator's Diagnostic Assessment

Area of personal skill or ability in teaching my children

Evaluate on a scale of 0 - 10
0=no ability/experience   10=mastered

Confidence to teach my students
0 1 2 3 4 5 6 7 8 9 10

Developing a clear philosophy and purpose for our educational program
0 1 2 3 4 5 6 7 8 9 10

Organizing the schooling environment
0 1 2 3 4 5 6 7 8 9 10

Managing my home so I can school
0 1 2 3 4 5 6 7 8 9 10

Planning ahead
0 1 2 3 4 5 6 7 8 9 10

Planning overall curriculum
0 1 2 3 4 5 6 7 8 9 10

Teaching and evaluating Bible
0 1 2 3 4 5 6 7 8 9 10

Teaching and evaluating reading
0 1 2 3 4 5 6 7 8 9 10

Teaching and evaluating writing
0 1 2 3 4 5 6 7 8 9 10

Teaching and evaluating history (geography, social studies, government, etc.)
0 1 2 3 4 5 6 7 8 9 10

Teaching and evaluating health and sciences
0 1 2 3 4 5 6 7 8 9 10

Teaching and evaluating the arts
0 1 2 3 4 5 6 7 8 9 10

Teaching and evaluating physical education
0 1 2 3 4 5 6 7 8 9 10

Teaching several grade levels at a time (if applicable)
0 1 2 3 4 5 6 7 8 9 10

Disciplining myself to complete school work
0 1 2 3 4 5 6 7 8 9 10

Disciplining my children to complete school work
0 1 2 3 4 5 6 7 8 9 10

Meeting each child's individual needs
0 1 2 3 4 5 6 7 8 9 10

Setting goals and objectives
0 1 2 3 4 5 6 7 8 9 10

Finding enjoyment in home schooling
0 1 2 3 4 5 6 7 8 9 10

Knowing my state requirements for my home-schooling program
0 1 2 3 4 5 6 7 8 9 10

Being informed and aware of current issues that could affect my home-schooling program
0 1 2 3 4 5 6 7 8 9 10

Creating and following a school schedule
0 1 2 3 4 5 6 7 8 9 10

Planning special activities (ie., field trips, cooperative study classes, library, etc.)
0 1 2 3 4 5 6 7 8 9 10

Diagnostic Reading Checklist

Student Name_____ Date_____

Reading Process	Frequently	Occasionally	Comments
Word Identification Strategies			
I. Reading Intention:			
Reads for meaning (comprehension)			
II. Predicting:			
Uses context clues to predict			
Rejects unsatisfactory predictions			
Integrates meaning			
III. Attention:			
Able to take whole sections of text (in contrast to word by word reading)			
Omits words in text			
Transposes words in text			
Adds words in text			

Substitutes words
    Graphic similarity
    Semantic similarity
    Sound similarity
    Grammatical similarity
    Changes meaning			

IV. When In Difficulty:			
Reads on to the end of a sentence			
Rereads sentence			
Uses initial letters as clues			
Uses pictorial clues			
Waits for help			
Quits			

Reading Process	Frequently	Occasionally	Comments
V. Synthesizing: Selects cues Blends words parts			
VI. Monitoring: Self-corrects			
READING PRODUCT: Comprehension			
VII. Prediction: Predicts story information Predicts story sequence (What might happen . . .)			

VIII. Analyzing/
Associating:
 	
Can retell story or
 information in own
 words
 	
Can recognize or infer:
    Main idea
    Details
    Character development
 	
Can recognize or infer:
    Sequence
    Cause and effect
    Comparison
 	
Can make judgments of:
    Values
    Reality and fantasy
    Fact and opinion
 	
Can appreciate an author's
skill			

Student Reading Inventory

Name _____ **Date**_____

My Reading

Evaluate on a scale of 0 - 10
0=not very much   10=very much

I like to read.	0 1 2 3 4 5 6 7 8 9 10
I am a good reader.	0 1 2 3 4 5 6 7 8 9 10
I am a fast reader.	0 1 2 3 4 5 6 7 8 9 10
I understand what I read by myself.	0 1 2 3 4 5 6 7 8 9 10
I understand what someone else reads to me.	0 1 2 3 4 5 6 7 8 9 10
The things I read are interesting.	0 1 2 3 4 5 6 7 8 9 10
I have a lot of books.	0 1 2 3 4 5 6 7 8 9 10
I like to tell others about the things I read about.	0 1 2 3 4 5 6 7 8 9 10

My favorite book is _____

My favorite author is _____

My favorite type of reading material is _____

My favorite time to read is_____

My favorite place to read is_____

My favorite thing to read about is _____

The last two books I read with someone else were _____

_____

_____

The last two books I read by myself were _____

_____

_____

Something I would like to read more is _____

_____

Teacher Notes: _____

_____

_____

_____

_____

Diagnostic Writing Checklist

Student Name _____ Date _____

Writing Features	Frequently	Occasionally	Not Enough Information	Comments

I. Organizational Features:
 	
Sequence of ideas/details
 	
Cause and effect
 	
Transitions
 	
Introductions
  (i.e. beginnings)
 	
Conclusions
  (i.e. endings)				

II. Developmental Features: Sentence sense Story sense Moral sense Topic depth Risk taking (Does the writer experiment, try new things?)				

III. Sentence Features:
 	
Simple sentences
 	
Compounding (combining sentences together)
 	
Variety:
   in beginnings
   in endings
   in length
 	
Organization into paragraphs				

Writing Features	Frequently	Occasionally	Not Enough Information	Comments
IV. Stylistic Features: Literal language Images Metaphors Comparisons/similes Vivid vocabulary Detailed descriptions Sentence variety				

V. Mechanical Features:
 	
Punctuation
 	
Capitalization
 	
Possessives
 	
Contractions
 	
Subject-verb agreement
 	
Tense agreement
   (past, present, future. . .)
 	
Verb endings
 	
Spelling
   (phonetic,
   conventional)				

Student Writing Inventory

Name _____ **Date** _____

My Reading

Evaluate on a scale of 0 - 10

0=not very much   10=very much

I like to write.	0 1 2 3 4 5 6 7 8 9 10
I am a good writer.	0 1 2 3 4 5 6 7 8 9 10
Writing is an important skill.	0 1 2 3 4 5 6 7 8 9 10
I like to show my writing to others.	0 1 2 3 4 5 6 7 8 9 10
The things I write are interesting.	0 1 2 3 4 5 6 7 8 9 10
Others can read and understand my writing.	0 1 2 3 4 5 6 7 8 9 10
I write a lot.	0 1 2 3 4 5 6 7 8 9 10

What I'm best at writing is _____

I think writing is important because _____

The kind of writing I like to do most is _____

My favorite time to write is_____

My favorite place to write is_____

My favorite thing to write about is _____

The last writing I did was_____

To become a better writer I need help with _____

Something I would like to write is _____

Teacher Notes: _____

_____

_____

_____

_____

_____

_____

OBSERVATION NOTES

Keep this list in a convenient location and add to it throughout the day or week. Anytime you make a "mental note" it should be added to your observation notes. Observe not just the finished product in each area, but the attitude toward the subject, length of time needed to accomplish related tasks, mistakes which are repeatedly made, teacher and student likes and dislikes, how much time is devoted to the area of study, etc. This will help to fill in the gaps left by other diagnostic tools which are more academic in form and purpose.

Character

_____

_____

_____

_____

_____

_____

_____

_____

_____

_____

_____

_____

_____

_____

_____

_____

_____

_____

_____

_____

_____

_____

_____

OBSERVATION NOTES

Reading
(Aloud and silent)

OBSERVATION NOTES

Penmanship

Spelling

OBSERVATION NOTES

Writing

OBSERVATION NOTES

Mathematics

_____
_____
_____
_____
_____
_____
_____
_____
_____
_____
_____
_____
_____
_____
_____
_____
_____
_____
_____
_____
_____
_____
_____
_____
_____
_____
_____
_____
_____
_____
_____
_____
_____

OBSERVATION NOTES

Science

_____
_____
_____
_____
_____
_____
_____
_____
_____
_____
_____
_____
_____
_____
_____
_____
_____
_____
_____
_____
_____
_____
_____
_____
_____
_____
_____
_____

History/Social Studies

OBSERVATION NOTES

Fine Arts (Music, Art, Drama)

_____
_____
_____
_____
_____
_____
_____
_____
_____
_____
_____
_____
_____
_____
_____
_____
_____
_____
_____
_____
_____
_____
_____
_____
_____
_____
_____
_____

OBSERVATION NOTES

Health

_____
_____
_____
_____
_____
_____
_____
_____
_____
_____
_____
_____
_____
_____
_____

Physical Fitness

_____
_____
_____
_____
_____
_____
_____
_____
_____
_____
_____
_____
_____
_____
_____

OBSERVATION NOTES

Bible/Religious Training

_____
_____
_____
_____
_____
_____
_____
_____
_____
_____
_____
_____
_____
_____

Additional Areas of Observation

_____
_____
_____
_____
_____
_____
_____
_____
_____
_____
_____
_____
_____
_____
_____
_____
_____
_____

OBSERVATION NOTES

Additional Observations

OBSERVATION NOTES

Additional Observations

_____
_____
_____
_____
_____
_____
_____
_____
_____
_____
_____
_____
_____
_____
_____
_____
_____
_____
_____
_____
_____
_____
_____
_____
_____
_____
_____
_____
_____
_____
_____

Character Qualities

Student Name _____   Evaluation Period _____

Character Quality	Weak	Improving	Satisfactory	Excellent
Attentiveness				
Brotherly Love				
Contentment				
Courtesy				
Cooperation				
Dependability				
Diligence				
Following Directions				
Forgiving				
Friendliness				
Gentleness				
Helpfulness				
Honesty				
Humility				
Industriousness				
Integrity				
Kindness				
Neatness				
Obedience				
Perseverance				
Prudence				
Respectfulness				
Self-control				

Student Inventory

Name _____ **Age** _____ **Date** _____

Subject or Skill	Excellent	Very Good	Pretty Good	Just O.K.	Not Very Good	Doesn't Apply
Bible						
Reading aloud						
Reading silently						
Vocabulary						
Writing organization						
Writing punctuation						
Creative writing						
Grammar and parts of speech						
Spelling						
Math – overall						
Addition/Subtraction						
Subtraction/ Multiplication						
Fractions						
Decimals						
Percents						
Word problems						
History						
Government						
Geography						
Using maps, charts and graphs						
Using reference materials to do research						
Science						
Health						
Physical Fitness						
Art						
Music						
Drama						
Oral presentations						

EDUCATOR'S OBJECTIVES

OBJECTIVE	METHOD Be as specific as you can. List book titles, people's names, conventions, etc.	INTENDED COMPLETION

OBJECTIVES & EVALUATION FORM

Student Name _____   Evaluation Period _____

Specific Objectives	Mastered	Satisfactory Progress	Needs More Work	Not Addressed
Character Development				
Bible and Christian Training				
Language Arts (reading, phonics, grammar, composition, spelling, vocabulary, penmanship)				

OBJECTIVES & EVALUATION FORM
continued

Specific Objectives	Mastered	Satisfactory Progress	Needs More Work	Not Addressed
Arithmetic				
Art				
Music				
P.E./Health				
Life Skills				
Social Studies				
Science				

Junior and Senior High Level
Writing Assignments

Note: These writing activities may come from any area of the curriculum, or family life. It is not necessary to complete them in order. They may be incorporated into the curriculum over a period of two or three years depending upon when you begin.

Writing Project	Due Date	Date Completed
List		
Memo		
Journal		
Short Story		
Summary		
Observations		
Dialogue		
Sketch		
Report		
Book Review		
Movie Review		
News Article		
Friendly Letter		
Business Letter		
Letter to the Editor		
Poetry		
Essay: Autobiographical Incident		
Essay: First-Hand Biography		
Essay: Memoir		
Essay: Evaluation		
Essay: Problem-Solution		
Essay: Analysis/Speculation		

SCIENCE PROJECT
STUDENT TIMELINE

Activity	Due Date	Date Completed
Choose a topic in which you are interested. Write out your topic.		
Collect books, information, and reference materials to research your topic. List your research materials.		
Write a report summarizing your research.		
Make a list of everything you will need to do in order. Include all the supplies you will need to carry out your project.		
Write out the procedure for your experiment or demonstration.		
Write a hypothesis. What do you predict will happen?		
Gather your materials. Get everything ready to carry out your experiment or demonstration.		
Perform your experiment or practice your demonstration.		
Record your observations.		
What did you learn or find out by doing this experiment? Record your conclusions in writing.		
Compare your conclusions to your original hypothesis.		
Prepare your display. Present the information you collected in easy-to-read graphs or tables.		
Prepare a two to three-minute oral presentation.		

STUDENT PROJECT TIMELINE

May be used to guide students through projects in nearly any area of study.

Activity	Due Date	Date Completed

Course Outline

Course title _____ **School Year** _____

Activity	Points Received

Poetry Reading/Recitation Evaluation

Use this rubric for evaluating any oral reading or recitation, including scripture memorization, poetry, short story, or family read-aloud time.

Name_____

Beginning with confidence (poise)	1	2	3	4	5

Beginning with confidence (poise)   1   2   3   4   5

Pronouncing words well (articulation and enunciation)   1   2   3   4   5

Volume   1   2   3   4   5

Eye contact   1   2   3   4   5

Expression   1   2   3   4   5

Total Points Earned _____

Poetry Reading/Recitation Evaluation

Use this rubric for evaluating any oral reading or recitation, including scripture memorization, poetry, short story, or family read-aloud time.

Name_____   1   2   3   4   5

Beginning with confidence (poise)   1   2   3   4   5

Pronouncing words well (articulation and enunciation)   1   2   3   4   5

Volume   1   2   3   4   5

Eye contact   1   2   3   4   5

Expression

Total Points Earned _____

Public Speaking Evaluation

This form may be used to evaluate an oral presentation in any area of the curriculum.

Name	Topic/Title
Components of the Speech	*Points Possible/Given*
Detail	(10)
Organization	(10)
Poise	(10)
Preparation	(10)
Eye contact	(10)
Articulation	(10)
Expression	(10)
Persuasiveness	(20)
Beginning and ending with confidence	(10)
Total Points Earned	

Grading Scale: *Grade:* _____

90% = A

80% = B

70% = C

Below 70% you must repeat assignment.

Comments:

Public Speaking Course Evaluation

Name _____   **Evaluation Period** _____

Effort								**Total Points**
Assignments completed promptly								
Discussion								
Respect shown parent/instructor								
Shows ability to give & receive constructive comments								
Encouragement of other students (siblings apply)								
Preparation for presentations/discussions								
Follows directions								
Achievement								
Humor								
Reading/recitation								
Impromptu								
Expository speech w/visual aids								
Extemporaneous speaking								
Persuasive speaking								
Public speaking quiz								
Dramatic/humorous interpretation								
Final presentation								
Total Points								

_____ FAMILY'S APPROVED BOOK LIST

BOOK TITLE	AUTHOR	POINT VALUE

GRADING SCHEDULE:

_____ POINTS = A

_____ POINTS = B

_____ POINTS = C

_____ POINTS = D

For some students, this grading schedule is sufficient to give a grade for reading or literature, for others it would be still more helpful and present a more complete picture to average reading points with project points to determine the student's grade.

Reading Genres

Name _____   Date Due _____

Goal _____

Genre	Date	Title	Date	Title
Allegory				
Biography				
Essays and Editorials				
Fantasy				
Historical Fiction				
Instruction				
News				
Novels				
Parables and Fables				
Plays				
Poetry				
Propaganda				
Reference Books				
Reviews				
Science Fiction				
Short Stories				
Texts				
Travel				

INDEPENDENT READING CONTRACT

Choose projects from "Book Project Ideas" to assign for books to be read during the quarter/semester/year.

Name _____

APPROVED BOOKS & PROJECTS

<u>Book Title</u>	<u>Projects / Date Due</u>

STUDENT SIGNATURE/DATE _____

BOOK PROJECTS

(Teacher's Note: Choose projects from the "Book Project Ideas" section which seem appropriate to the literature selected.)

The following book projects have been assigned point values based upon completing them in a manner that demonstrates your highest level of creativity, skills, and abilities. Anything less than your best effort will result in point deductions.

PROJECTS

PROJECT DESCRIPTION	DATE DUE	POINTS POSSIBLE	POINTS EARNED

GRADING PERIOD: _____
GRADING SCHEDULE:
_____POINTS = A
_____POINTS = B
_____POINTS = C
_____POINTS = D

TOTAL POINTS
EARNED: _____

GRADE
EARNED: _____

Literature Project Syllabus

Name_____ Book Title _____

Date Due_____

Item	Points Possible/ Earned
* Read your book.	
* Record book title, author, illustrator, number of pages, and a brief summary of the story line on one page.	
Create a collage of highlights, symbols, settings, and important features of the story.	
Illustrate your favorite scene from the book. Incorporate as many details as possible.	
Pretend you are the main character in your story. Write a letter to someone telling about an important day or event in your life.	
Design a poster that would encourage people to read your book (like a poster advertising a movie that's just coming to the theater).	
Choose the most exciting, suspenseful, or dramatic excerpt from the book to read aloud to family or friends. Practice reading with as much feeling and expression as you can.	
Cook or bake a special food mentioned in the story. Write about your experience.	
Design a postcard that one of the characters in the story might send to someone they know. Draw a scene on the front and write on the back.	
Dress up like one of the characters in the story. Prepare to give a two to three-minute presentation about yourself including important information from the story.	
TOTAL POINTS EARNED	

Student Writing Sample

Name _____   Date _____

Writing Topic (Choose one from pages 28-29 or create your own.)

_____

_____

Directions

Write an essay about the topic described above. Use as many descriptive words as you can, so the person reading your essay will understand why it is important or interesting. Be sure to use correct punctuation, spelling, and grammar.

_____

_____

_____

_____

_____

_____

_____

_____

_____

_____

_____

_____

_____

_____

_____

_____

_____

_____

_____

Our Family's Favorite Writing Prompts

Writing Assignment

Assignment: _____

_____

Length: (in words, paragraphs or pages) _____

Promptness: (10) Due Date _____ Time _____ a.m. p.m.

Neatness: (10) _____ manuscript _____cursive _____typed

Content: (20) Specific information to be included

_____
_____
_____
_____
_____
_____

Expression: (20) Vary sentence beginnings. Add descriptive words to make your paper more interesting.

Mechanics: (20) Emphasis for this paper is upon _____

_____
_____

Graphics: (20) Include –
Cover _____ Illustration _____ Chart _____ Graph _____ Other _____
Graphics should illustrate _____

_____
_____

WRITING CRITIQUE
(Attach to _all_ written assignments.)

Name_____ Due Date and Time_____

Actual Completion Date and Time _____

	POINTS POSSIBLE	POINTS RECEIVED
PROMPTNESS		
NEATNESS		
CONTENT (information)		
EXPRESSION (vocabulary, description . . .)		
MECHANICS (punctuation)		
GRAPHICS (cover/charts/illustrations)		
TOTAL POINTS RECEIVED		
EXTRA CREDIT		
FINAL POINTS		

GRADE: _____

CRITIQUE:_____

_____

_____

_____

_____

_____

Handwriting Critique

Student Name _____   Year _____

Handwriting Features *(Scale 1-5: 5=perfect)*	Assessment Date						
Posture (back, feet, forearms are in proper position during writing)							
Pencil Hold (pencil resting properly in relaxed hand)							
Paper Position (student places paper in correct position for writing)							
Stroke Direction (moves pencil in proper direction to form each letter)							
Shape (each letter is formed correctly)							
Size (properly sized in proportion to each other, upper and lowercase)							
Slant (Slope) (varies with writing style, but should be consistent)							
Spacing (proper spacing within and between words)							
Speed (student maintains a consistent, comfortable rate of speed)							
Height (tall and short letters begin and end where they should)							
Consistency (consistent writing)							
Overall neatness and legibility							
Letters that need work next							

Note: Use with "Informal Handwriting Assessment" shown on page 35. Modify or add your own features based on your own handwriting goals for your student and the goals of the curriculum you are using.

Writing Mechanics and Punctuation

Student Name _____   Evaluation Period _____

Mechanics are evaluated within the context of written work that is reviewed on each of the assessment dates. You may choose to evaluate mechanics of writing more or less often depending upon the student's writing ability and the skills and concepts being introduced.

Skill	Assessment Date						
Written Work Evaluated							
Mechanics:							
Capitals (20)							
▪ Italics or Underlines:(5) ▪ Titles of books ▪ Proper names ▪ Foreign words and phrases ▪ Words named as words ▪ Emphasis							
Abbreviations (5)							
Numbers - Usage in writing (5)							
Word Divisions: (5) ▪ Ends-beginnings of lines ▪ Compound words ▪ Hyphenated words							
Proper Verb Form: (20) ▪ Subject-verb agreement ▪ Past/present/future ▪ Singular/plural							
Pronoun-Antecedent Agreement (10)							
Complete Sentences (10) (no fragments or run-ons)							
Proper Word Usage (20)							
Paragraphs (10) ▪ Related sentences are grouped ▪ Indentations are used appropriately							
Spelling (20)							

Writing Mechanics and Punctuation, page 2

Skill	Assessment Date						
Punctuation:							
End Punctuation: (20) ▪ Period ▪ Question mark ▪ Exclamation point							
Commas: (20) ▪ Dates, addresses, place names, long numbers ▪ Introductory phrases and clauses ▪ Three or more items in a series ▪ With quotations ▪ To set apart phrases ▪ To set apart the person being addressed							
Quotation Marks (5)							
Semicolon: (5) ▪ Long items in a series ▪ Joining main clauses ▪ Setting apart long main clauses							
Apostrophes: (10) ▪ Possessives ▪ Contractions ▪ Plural possessives							
Other Punctuation: (10) ▪ Colon ▪ Dash, hyphen, slash ▪ Parentheses, brackets ▪ Ellipsis mark ( )							
Total Points for This Writing Assessment Percentage Score (Divide total points by 200) *(Can be translated into letter grade.)*							

Note: 200 points possible. Deduct one point for each error in the appropriate category as you evaluate the student's written work. If a writing feature does not apply, omit the category. For example, if the student does not yet use any of the "other punctuation," omit the category and adjust the points accordingly. You may add points to another category or simply account for the difference when you average the score. If you are placing a great deal of emphasis on a specific writing skill such as the use of dialogue in a story, you may choose to give it more weight as there will be more opportunity for error in the student's work. You might deduct two points per error for a skill that was just taught to give it more attention, as well.

ORAL PRESENTATION
STUDENT GUIDELINES

Prepare a short story or poem. Your reading or recitation must meet the following requirements:

+ _____ minutes in length.
+ The subject of the poem or story must be clear.
+ It must be a published work.
+ You may read or recite but be sure you are familiar enough with the content to use as much expression as possible.
+ It is to be presented at the following date and time:_____

Your presentation will be evaluated for:

Requirement	Points Possible	Points Earned
Being prepared on time		
Beginning and ending with confidence		
Poise		
Eye contact		
Articulation		
Expression		
Projection (volume)		
Appropriate theme		
Staying within the time allotted		
Total		

Your grade will be based on points earned. You are not being compared to anyone else. You are being compared to the best that you are capable of in each area. *Your preparation* will determine the quality of your presentation.

Grading Scale: 75 points = C+
95 points = A .   70 points = C
90 points = A-   Below this point you obviously did not prepare
85 points = B   and will be required to present this material at
80 points = B-   the following date and time_____

Format For One Page Essay
Emphasis on *Content*

Title (Appropriate for the Essay topic) (10 points)
I. Introductory Paragraph
  A. Topic Sentence - State what the paper is about. (15)
  B. Three things you intend to say about the topic
    1. (5)
    2. (5)
    3. (5)
II. Body of the Paper
  A. Paragraph 2
    Three things about point #1
    1. (5)
    2. (5)
    3. (5)
  B. Paragraph 3
    Three things about point #2
    1. (5)
    2. (5)
    3. (5)
  C. Paragraph 4
    Three things about point #3
    1. (5)
    2. (5)
    3. (5)
III. Summary of the Paper (15)
  A. Draw a conclusion, e.g., "Something I learned in this study . . ."
    (restate in your own words), *and/or*
  B. Summarize your points, *and/or*
  C. Restate the topic sentence in different words

Student Notes:
- Your points should be three things about the topic that are related but different.
- You need to say three things about each point that are related but different.
- A clearly stated topic sentence will make the entire paper easier to follow.
- Vary sentence beginnings to make your paper more interesting.

Purposes for Writing

Note: These writing activities might come from any area of the curriculum, or family life. It is not necessary to complete them in order. They might be incorporated into the curriculum over a period of two or three years depending upon when you begin.

Writing Project	Due Date	Date Completed
List		
Memo		
Journal		
Short Story		
Summary		
Observations		
Dialogue		
Sketch		
Report		
Book Review		
Movie Review		
News Article		
Friendly Letter		
Business Letter		
Letter to the Editor		
Poetry		
Essay: Autobiographical Incident		
Essay: First-Hand Biography		
Essay: Memoir		
Essay: Evaluation		
Essay: Problem-Solution		
Essay: Analysis/Speculation		

RESEARCH PROJECT EVALUATION

Name_____ Due Date and Time_____
Project Name _____
Actual Completion Date and Time _____

	POINTS POSSIBLE	POINTS RECEIVED
PROMPTNESS		
NEATNESS		
CONTENT (information)		
EXPRESSION (vocabulary, description . . .)		
MECHANICS (punctuation)		
GRAPHICS (cover/charts/illustrations)		
BIBLIOGRAPHY (references and format)		
EXTRA CREDIT		
FINAL POINTS		
GRADE EARNED		

GRADING SCALE: COMMENTS:_____

_____points = A   _____
_____points = A-   _____
_____points = B+   _____
_____points = B   _____
_____points = B-   _____

SCIENCE PROJECT EVALUATION

Student's Name _____   Year in School _____

Project Name _____   Due Date _____

Points

	1	2	3	4	5
Originality and Creativity Idea, approach, and method show original and creative thinking.	1	2	3	4	5
Scientific Thought Knowledge of the subject of study is demonstrated ,and scientific accuracy is evident.	1	2	3	4	5
Work and Organization Project indicates thought, time, and care in preparation and organization	1	2	3	4	5
Visual Presentation Exhibit is neat and attractive. Project is clearly and thoroughly presented.	1	2	3	4	5
Oral Presentation Project is clearly explained to the evaluator.	1	2	3	4	5
Total Points Earned _____					
Grade Earned _____					

Grading Scale: _____ points = A   _____ points = B-
                _____ points = A-   _____ points = C+
                _____ points = B+   _____ points = C
                _____ points = B   _____ points = C-

Physical Education

Name_____ **Evaluation Period** _____

Activity	Time spent in _____ minute intervals												

Math Skills Checklist

Student Name _____

Evaluation Period _____   Level _____

Concept or Skill	Introduced	Practicing	Mastered	Not Addressed

Math Basics

Name _____

Evaluation Period _____

	10 min	8 min	6 min	5 min	4 min	3 min	2 min	1 min
Addition Facts: 100 facts, single digit								
Subtraction Facts: 100 facts, single digit								
Addition Facts: 50 facts, two-digit (no re-grouping)								
Subtraction Facts: 50 facts, two-digit (no re-grouping)								
Addition Facts: 50 facts, two-digit (re-grouping)								
Subtraction Facts: 50 facts, two-digit, (re-grouping)								
Multiplication Facts: to 5 x 5								
Multiplication Facts: to 10 x 10								
Multiplication Facts: to 12 x 12								
Division Facts: to 5								
Division Facts: to 8								
Division Facts: to 10								
Division Facts: to 12								
Fractions: +,- with like denominators								
Fractions: simplify								
Fractions: +,- without common denominators								
Fractions: multiply and reduce to lowest terms								
Fractions: divide								
Decimals: +,-,x,÷								
Convert decimals to fractions								
Percentages: convert to fractions and decimals								

ARITHMETIC LESSONS

BOOK TITLE _____   STUDENT NAME _____
PUBLISHER_____   GRADING PERIOD _____
LEVEL _____

LESSON #	DATE	TIME SPENT	% SCORE	LESSON #	DATE	TIME SPENT	% SCORE

ARITHMETIC TEST SCORES

STUDENT NAME_____ GRADING PERIOD_____

TEST #	DATE	TIME SPENT	% SCORE	TEST #	DATE	TIME SPENT	% SCORE
			AVERAGE				AVERAGE

AVERAGE LESSON SCORE (%) _____
(Add all lesson scores and divide
by the number of lessons)
AVERAGE TEST SCORE (%) _____

AVERAGE OF LESSON
AND TEST SCORES _____
GRADE _____
COMMENTS:_____

_____
_____
_____

Literature Unit Study

Activity *Choose the activities you want to do to receive the number of points needed for the grade you desire*	Method of Evaluation	Points Possible	Points Received
Read Book Title: _____			
Research Outline Topic: _____			
Glossary			
Essay. Compare and contrast two major issues, situations, or concepts from the book.			
Research Report: Topic: _____			
Write a biography about someone from the story or about the author.			
Oral Presentation			
Map: labeled and colored. The map must include_____ _____			
Total Score			

Grading Schedule:

_____ points = A
_____ points = B
_____ points = C
_____ points or below = Redo project

Teacher note: Refer to the "Geography Unit Study Sample" for help in designing a literature unit study.

Map Guidelines Label and color the following features on your map:	Points Possible	Points Received

Individualized Education Program (IEP)

General Information

Student Name _____ Grade _____ Sex: M ___ F ____

School Year _____ Birthdate _____

Parent/Guardian Names _____

Street Address _____

Mailing Address _____

Telephone: Home _____ Work _____

School Schedule: Traditional ____ Year Round ____

Special Needs: The student has ____ has not ___ been diagnosed with special needs.
If you checked "has," complete the "Special Education" page of the IEP.

This IEP includes the following:
Student Success Study Team Evaluation Forms from the following individuals:

Name	Relationship to student	Contact
_____	_____	_____
_____	_____	_____
_____	_____	_____
_____	_____	_____
_____	_____	_____
_____	_____	_____
_____	_____	_____

The following diagnostic and assessment tools were used in developing objectives for this term and are attached:

_____

_____

This IEP addresses the following areas of the student's development:

		Other
Reading ____	Math ____	
Spelling ____	Science ____	_____
Writing ____	History ____	_____
Reference ____	Physical Fitness ___	_____
Study Skills ____	Life Skills ____	_____
Organization Skills ____		_____

IEP completed by _____ Relationship to student _____

Mother's Signature _____ Father's Signature _____

Student Success Study Team
Individualized Education Program (IEP)

You have been asked to participate in this Student Success Study Team because you have participated in or observed some aspect of education and development for the following student: _____

Please complete the following information from your observations of this student to the best of your ability.

Teacher/Instructor/Observer Name: _____

Activities/Skills/Areas Observed: _____

_____

Present Levels of Performance

Strengths   Concerns

_____   _____
_____   _____
_____   _____
_____   _____
_____   _____
_____   _____
_____   _____
_____   _____
_____   _____

Significant Factors Contributing to Performance
(Social, Emotional, Health, Academic, Behavioral, Physical) Please be specific.

Strengths   Concerns

_____   _____
_____   _____
_____   _____
_____   _____
_____   _____
_____   _____
_____   _____
_____   _____

From my observations and interactions, I believe the following actions would help this student continue to progress: _____

_____
_____
_____

Signature _____   Date _____

Individualized Education Program (IEP)
Annual Goals and Methods

Name _____ **Grade** _____

Goal Setting Date _____ **Anticipated Completion Date** _____

These goals may be taken from a scope and sequence like the one included on page 16 or from the curriculum resources you have chosen for this school year.

Subject	Objective	Obj. Met	Method	Materials	Level

Individualized Education Program (IEP)
Annual Goals and Methods, page 2

Subject	Objective	Obj. Met	Method	Materials	Level

Individualized Education Program (IEP)
Special Education

Describe the disability: _____

Disability was diagnosed by (doctor/counsellor): _____

Date of diagnosis and method of diagnosis (tests used, etc.): _____

_____

What is the difference between his/her level of achievement and the level expected at his/her age? _____

_____

What sources, public or private, are currently being used to address this child's needs?

_____

_____

_____

Check all handicapping conditions which apply below:

☐ Mentally Retarded   ☐ Other Health Impaired
☐ Hard of Hearing   ☐ Blind
☐ Deaf   ☐ Multihandicapped
☐ Speech/Language Impaired   ☐ Autistic
☐ Visually Impaired   ☐ Traumatic Brain Injury
☐ Seriously Emotionally Disturbed   ☐ Specific Learning Disability:
☐ Orthopedically Impaired
                                     _____

Student needs the following equipment:

_____

_____

REFERENCE MATERIALS

List all reference materials used during the school year in any subject area. Include any materials—books, magazines, newspapers, audio, video, etc.—that were used for reference purposes.

Student Name _____ **School Year** _____

TITLE	AUTHOR/ PUBLISHER	TITLE	AUTHOR/ PUBLISHER

Oral Presentation Critique	
Name_____ Topic_____ Date Given_____	
Components of the Speech	**Points Possible/ Given**
Beginning with confidence	(5)
Use of interesting details	(10)
Organization	(15)
Appropriate use of visual aids	(10)
Poise	(10)
Preparation	(15)
Eye contact	(10)
Articulation	(10)
Expression	(10)
Ending with confidence	(5)
Total Points Earned	(100)
Comments:	

Oral Presentation Critique	
Name_____ Topic_____ Date Given_____	
Components of the Speech	**Points Possible/ Given**
Beginning with confidence	(5)
Use of interesting details	(10)
Organization	(15)
Appropriate use of visual aids	(10)
Poise	(10)
Preparation	(15)
Eye contact	(10)
Articulation	(10)
Expression	(10)
Ending with confidence	(5)
Total Points Earned	(100)
Comments:	

Critical Thinking Skills

Name _____ Date _____

Topic _____

Knowledge:

_____

_____

Comprehension:

_____

_____

Application:

_____

_____

Analysis:

_____

_____

Synthesis:

_____

_____

Evaluation:

_____

_____

Forms Index

Sample Form	Page
Approved Book List	165
Arithmetic Lessons	185
Arithmetic Test Scores	186
Book Projects	168
Character Qualities Review	153
Course Outline	161
Critical Thinking Skills	196
Diagnostic Reading Checklist	134-35
Diagnostic Writing Checklist	137-38
Educator's Diagnostic Survey	133
Educator's Objectives	155
Format for One-page Essay	178
Handwriting Critique	174
Independent Reading Contract	167
Individualized Education Program (IEP)	189
IEP Annual Goals and Methods	191-92
IEP Special Education	193
IEP Student Success Study Team	190
Junior and Senior High Level Writing Assignments	158
Literature Project	169
Literature Unit Study	187
Map Guidelines	188
Math Basics	184
Math Skills Checklist	183
Objectives and Evaluation Form	156-57
Observation Notes	140-52
Oral Presentation Critique	195
Oral Presentation Student Guidelines	177

Forms Index

Sample Form	Page
Physical Education Record	182
Poetry Reading/Recitation Evaluation	162
Public Speaking Course Evaluation	164
Public Speaking Evaluation	163
Purposes for Writing	179
Reading Genres	166
Reference Materials	194
Research Project Evaluation	180
Science Project Evaluation	181
Science Project Student Timeline	159
Student Inventory	154
Student Reading Inventory	136
Student Writing Inventory	139
Student Writing Sample	170
Writing Assignment	172
Writing Critique	173
Writing Mechanics and Punctuation	175-76
Writing Prompts	171

ABOUT THE AUTHOR

Homeschool mom, tutor, credentialed teacher and former public school administrator, Teresa Moon holds a Master of Arts degree in Curriculum and Instruction. A nationally featured seminar speaker and author, Teresa conducts workshops around the country to encourage home educators and leaders in a lifestyle of biblical education, building their confidence using insight from her experience as an educator and sharing practical helps for teaching their children. Teresa has inspired students to think critically and speak persuasively, producing winning student speakers at state and national competitions. Teresa leads her staff of trained student instructors, conducting "Communicators For Christ" conferences around the United States, to encourage Christian students and their parents to refine the skills of biblical communication and to articulate truth. She is the author of two books, *Evaluating For Excellence* and *Public Speaking: lessons for the Christian student (and teacher)* along with several curriculum supplements.

Those wishing to contact Teresa Moon about speaking engagements may contact her at:
Harvest Educational Services
1370 Trancas St., #376, Napa, CA 94558
(707) 254-7344
email: harvestca@pobox.com